a **Biggin Hill** ng
01959 574468

THE LONDON BOROUGH
www.bromley.gov.uk

Please return/renew this item
by the last date shown.
Books may also be renewed by
phone and Internet

D0230573

CAMBRIDGE

CAMBRIDGE UNIVERSITY PRESS
Cambridge, New York, Melbourne, Madrid, Cape Town, Singapore, São Paulo

Cambridge University Press
The Edinburgh Building, Cambridge CB2 2RU, UK

www.cambridge.org
Information on this title: www.cambridge.org/9780521520607

First published 2004
3rd printing 2006

Printed in Singapore by C.O.S Printers Pte Ltd

A catalogue record for this publication is available from the British Library

ISBN-13 978-0-521-52060-7 paperback
ISBN-10 0-521-52060-6 paperback

Illustrations by Enrico Sallustio

Contents

Introduction			v
Glossary			vi
Unit	1	Adjectives 1: meaning	1
Unit	2	Adjectives 2: adjectives ending in *-ing* / *-ed*	3
Unit	3	Adjectives 3: making adjectives negative	5
Unit	4	Adjectives 4: adding *-er* / *-est* to an adjective	7
Unit	5	Adverbs 1: meaning	9
Unit	6	Adverbs 2: forming adverbs	10
Unit	7	Adverbs 3: using adverbs	12
Unit	8	American and British spelling	14
Unit	9	Apostrophes 1: to show omission	17
Unit	10	Apostrophes 2: to show possession	19
Unit	11	*as* and *like*	23
Unit	12	Capital letters	25
Unit	13	Colons (:)	27
Unit	14	Commas 1: when to pause	29
Unit	15	Commas 2: how to pause	31
Unit	16	Commas 3: the comma and relative clauses	34
Unit	17	Common spelling errors	36
Unit	18	Comparisons: comparatives and superlatives	39
Unit	19	Concord: subject-verb agreement	42
Unit	20	Dashes (–)	46
Unit	21	Direct speech: showing what someone has said	48
Unit	22	Emphatic English	50
Unit	23	Formal English	52
Unit	24	Greek and Latin roots	54
Unit	25	Homophones: words that sound alike	56
Unit	26	Hyphens (-)	59
Unit	27	Informal English 1: informal speech	61
Unit	28	Informal English 2: spoken and written English	63
Unit	29	Informal English 3: helpful hints	66
Unit	30	Irregular verbs	68
Unit	31	Loan words	72
Unit	32	Loose English	74

Unit 33	Negative prefixes	77
Unit 34	Nouns 1: noun endings	79
Unit 35	Nouns 2: formation and spelling	83
Unit 36	Passive voice	86
Unit 37	Plain English	90
Unit 38	Plurals	92
Unit 39	Prepositions	95
Unit 40	Regular verbs in the past	99
Unit 41	Relative pronouns: *who, which, whose, whom*	101
Unit 42	Semicolons (;)	103
Unit 43	Spoken and written English	104
Unit 44	Starting and finishing a sentence	107
Unit 45	Suffixes	109
Unit 46	Tricky verbs	112
Unit 47	Unnecessary words	114
Unit 48	Word endings 1: *-ible* and *-able*	117
Unit 49	Word endings 2: *-ent* and *-ant*	119
Unit 50	Word endings 3: *-ary, -ery, -ory, -ury*	121
Unit 51	Word endings 4: *-us, -ous, -ious, -eous*	123
Unit 52	Words 1: one word or maybe / may be two?	125
Unit 53	Words 2: two words in one	127
	Appendix 1	
	Confusing words 1	129
	Confusing words 2	131
	Confusing words 3	133
	Confusing words 4	135
	Appendix 2	
	Words ending in *-k, -ck,* and *-ke*	137
	Appendix 3	
	Some problems of usage	139
Knowledge check		141
Answer key		181
Knowledge check answer key		196

Introduction

Users of English often have doubts about the accuracy and appropriateness of the language they are using. *English Basics: a companion to grammar and writing* is a self-study reference and practice book that aims to help users negotiate tricky areas of English. It also gives help with various aspects of writing, especially punctuation and spelling – two areas of written English that are often neglected in books on usage.

This book can be used by students at high school/higher secondary/college level, teachers, trainee teachers, trainers and anyone who needs to use English with a high degree of competence in their jobs.

Each unit is divided into reference and task sections. The tasks are designed to test users' knowledge of a particular point and assess strengths and weaknesses. A *Knowledge check* section with more in-depth exercises is included at the back of the book. This provides opportunities for extension, revision and consolidation of particular points.

Entries have been arranged in alphabetical order for easy reference. Where required, potential areas of difficulty or confusion have been highlighted. Usage points are amply illustrated with examples.

Glossary

Before using this book, you should make sure that you are familiar with the following grammatical terms printed in **bold**:

1 The English alphabet has 26 letters, comprising five **vowels** (A, E, I, O, U) and 21 **consonants**.

2 A **verb** is a 'doing', 'being' or 'having' word (denoting action, occurrence, state or experience). The **subject** of a verb is the 'doer' of the action. The **object** of a verb is the 'receiver' of the action. The two words in italics are examples of verbs: 'Kirsty *plays* three instruments. She *is* a very talented girl.'

3 A **noun** is a word used to denote or name a person, place, thing, quality or an act. A **compound noun** (e.g. rainfall) is a noun made up of two words or more.

4 A **pronoun** (e.g. he, she, it) replaces a noun.

5 An **adjective** describes a noun or pronoun. A **compound adjective** (e.g. good-looking) is made up of two words or more.

6 The primary function of an **adverb** is to tell us more about a verb (e.g. she *easily* passed the exam) or an adjective (e.g. it was a *really* easy exam). An **adverbial phrase** (e.g. all of a sudden) is a group of words that acts in the same way as an adverb.

7 **Prepositions** are words like *in*, *on*, *from*, *at* and *by* which are usually (but not always) found before a noun or pronoun.

8 **Conjunctions** are linking words such as *and*, *but*, *or*, *if* and *when* that are used to join other words, groups of words or parts of a sentence.

9 A **sentence** is a set of words grouped together in such a way as to make complete sense. In written English, a sentence begins with a capital letter and ends with a full stop (.), a question mark (?) or an exclamation mark (!).

10 A **clause** is a group of words containing a verb. The following sentence consists of two clauses: 'Although I am very fond of you, I don't want to marry you.'

In the sentence above, *I don't want to marry you* is the **main clause**. A main clause can stand on its own as an independent sentence. *Although I am very fond of you* is a **subordinate** (or **dependent**) **clause**. A subordinate clause cannot stand on its own as an independent sentence.

11 **Participles** are verb forms used primarily in combination with the verbs *to be* and *to have* to form compound tenses e.g. I am *eating.* (present participle) / I have *eaten.* (past participle)

1 Adjectives 1: meaning

a An adjective is a word that describes something or someone. The words *big* and *nice* are adjectives.

b Sometimes it is difficult to remember how to spell an adjective because of the way it is pronounced. Such words need to be learnt by heart.
   e.g. tough / rough / straight (pronounced 'tuff' / 'ruff' / 'strait')

c Some common adjectives cause spelling problems because there are double letters within the word. Again, such words need to be learnt by heart.
   e.g. sorry, possible, difficult, different, necessary, horrible, terrible

d There are, however, some spelling rules which will make life easier for you when using adjectives.

   - When the word *full* is added to another word, the last *-l* is dropped. That is why there is only one *-l* at the end of such adjectives as *careful, beautiful, awful, painful...*

   - When we add *-y* to a word ending in *-e*, the *-e* usually disappears.
     e.g. grease – greasy; noise – noisy; rose – rosy; scare – scary

   - When we add *-y* to a one-syllable word that ends in one vowel + consonant, the consonant is doubled.
     e.g. sun – sunny; fog – foggy; fun – funny

Note: There is no *-e* in front of the *-y*. Very few adjectives end in *-ey* (e.g. grey). Most words that end in *-ey* are <u>nouns</u> (e.g. monkey, turkey, donkey) rather than adjectives.

Look at the jokes below. How many adjectives can you find? Underline them.

1 Secretary: What silly fool put these flowers on my desk?
  Boss: I did.
  Secretary: Oh, aren't they lovely!

2 Customer: This chicken is terrible. I want the manager.
  Waiter: I'm sorry, sir. He's not on the menu.

(Answers: page 182)

2 Adjectives 2: adjectives ending in *-ing* / *-ed*

a Adjectives may end in *-ing* or *-ed*.
   e.g. This lesson is boring. / I am bored.

b To form such adjectives, we apply the same rules used for forming verbs ending in *-ing* or *-ed*. (see pages 99, 109)

   When adding *-ing*, remember:
   • we drop the *-e* if the word ends in a consonant + *-e*
     e.g. amuse – amusing

   • *-y* does not change
     e.g. worry – worrying

   When adding *-ed*, remember:
   • if there is already an *-e*, just add *-d*
     e.g. amuse – amused

   • *-y* + *-ed* becomes *-ied* if there is a consonant in front of the *-y*
     e.g. worry – worried

c Adjectives ending in *-ing* are often used to describe what someone or something is like.
   e.g. It is interesting. / He is good-looking. / He is charming.

d Adjectives ending in *-ed* are often used to describe feelings.
   e.g. I am pleased. / I am shocked. / He looks frightened.

e Certain adjectives are so common that you should make absolutely sure that you do not misspell them. The following adjectives should be learnt by heart:
   e.g. annoying – annoyed; boring – bored; depressing – depressed; disappointing – disappointed; disgusting – disgusted; embarrassing – embarrassed; exciting – excited; frightening – frightened; horrifying – horrified; shocking – shocked; surprising – surprised; terrifying – terrified; worrying – worried; satisfying – satisfied

3

> *Note:* If you say 'I am bored', it means that you find something not very interesting. If, on the other hand, you say 'I am boring', it means that you make other people bored.

TASK

Complete the sentences by rewriting each word in brackets so that it ends in either *-ing* or *-ed*.

1 I found the book very (bore).

2 I'm not (interest) in sport.

3 It's an (amaze) thing.

4 He wasn't (satisfy) with what I said.

5 It was quite an (amuse) film.

6 I'm sorry, but I'm not (amuse). That wasn't funny.

7 She is (annoy) with me because I didn't help her.

8 What's that (annoy) noise?

9 This report is really (please).

10 She had a (worry) expression on her face.

(Answers: page 182)

3 Adjectives 3: making adjectives negative

a Many adjectives can be made negative by adding a *prefix* to them. A prefix is a letter or group of letters added to the beginning of a word to make a new word.

e.g. happy – <u>un</u>happy (*un-* = a negative prefix)

b Which negative prefix goes with which adjective?

- *ir-*, *il-*, *im-*
  These three prefixes follow a particular pattern with some adjectives.

- The prefix *ir-* is added to certain adjectives beginning with *r*.
  e.g. (ir)regular; (ir)responsible; (ir)relevant

  Some exceptions: (un)reliable; (un)reasonable

- The prefix *il-* is added to certain adjectives beginning with *l*.
  e.g. (il)logical; (il)legal; (il)literate

  Some exceptions: (un)lucky; (un)limited

- The prefix *im-* is added to certain adjectives beginning with *m* or *p*.

  e.g. (im)moral; (im)mature; (im)possible; (im)polite

  Some exceptions: (un)popular; (un)pleasant

- *in-*, *dis-*, *un-*

  These three prefixes do not follow a predictable pattern. The commonest prefix is *un-*. Adjectives taking *in-* and *dis-* should be learnt by heart.

  e.g. • (in)accurate; (in)expensive; (in)effective; (in)efficient; (in)capable; (in)secure

  • (dis)loyal; (dis)honest; (dis)respectful; (dis)agreeable

  • (un)occupied; (un)necessary; (un)official; (un)acceptable

---

TASK

Write down one word in place of the two given. In each case, you will have to supply an adjective beginning with *il-*, *im-*, *in-*, *ir-*, *un-* or *dis-*.

1 not possible =

2 not legal =

3 not regular =

4 not honest =

5 not usual =

6 not important =

7 not necessary =

8 not mature =

9 not patient =

10 not visible =

(Answers: page 182)

4 Adjectives 4: adding *-er* / *-est* to an adjective

a If an adjective ends in *-er*, this tells us that a comparison is being made.

    e.g. He is <u>taller</u> than <u>his mother</u>.

b If an adjective ends in *-est*, this tells us that a particular person or thing is being singled out from a group of people or things.

    e.g. Paul is the <u>tallest</u> boy in the class.

c We add *-er* or *-est* to one-syllable adjectives (e.g. fat, thin) and to two-syllable adjectives ending in *-y* (e.g. easy, pretty). For most other two-syllable adjectives and all polysyllabic adjectives, (as in d below) we use *more* and *most*.

    e.g. This chair is <u>more</u> comfortable than that one.

           This is the <u>most</u> interesting book I have ever read.

d We apply the following rules when adding *-er* or *-est* to an adjective:

- For words of one syllable ending in *-e*, just add *-r* or *-st.*
  e.g. large – larger – largest; safe – safer – safest

- For words of one syllable ending in one vowel + consonant, the final consonant is doubled.
  e.g. fit – fitter – fittest; thin – thinner – thinnest

- For words of one syllable ending in two vowels + consonant, the final consonant is <u>not</u> doubled.
  e.g. great – greater – greatest; cool – cooler – coolest

- When *-er* or *-est* is added to an adjective ending in a consonant + *-y*, the *-y* becomes *-i.*
  e.g. easy – easier – easiest; pretty – prettier – prettiest; lazy – lazier – laziest; dry – drier – driest

> *Note:* All adjectives ending in *-est* are normally preceded by the definite article *the.*

Decide whether each adjective in brackets should end in -*er* or -*est*.
Then write out each sentence.

1 "What's the (cheap) and (easy) way to see the world?"
   "Buy an altas!"

2 "What is the (dirty) word in the world?"
   "Pollution!"

3 "Which word grows (small) when you add letters to it?"
   "I don't know."
   "Short. When you add -*er* to short, it becomes (short)!"

4 Teacher: Do fish grow fast?
   Waqar: I'll say they do! My dad caught one last week and it gets
             (big) every time he talks about it.

5 Teacher: What is the (large) species of mouse in the world?
   David: A hippopotamouse!

(Answers: page 182)

5 Adverbs 1: meaning

a An adverb adds extra information to a verb (i.e. it modifies a verb).
   e.g. He smiled.
       He smiled <u>nervously</u>.

b An adverb can strengthen or weaken an adjective.
   e.g. He is ill.   I was surprised.
       He is <u>seriously</u> ill.   I was <u>slightly</u> surprised.

c An adverb can accompany a whole phrase or sentence.
   e.g. Nobody was injured.
       <u>Fortunately</u>, nobody was injured.

TASK

I Underline the adverbs in the following sentences:

   1 My younger sister sings beautifully.

   2 The old man drove carefully.

   3 The tall woman spoke quietly and calmly.

   4 It rained heavily.

II Correct the following sentences:

   1 He drove slow.

   2 I was real glad to see her.

   3 They beat us easy.

   4 He spoke to her as gentle as possible.

(Answers: page 182)

9

6   Adverbs 2: forming adverbs

a   An adverb ending in *-ly* is formed from an adjective.
    e.g.   slow – slowly; quick – quickly

b   If an adjective already ends in *-l*, we will end up with *-lly*.
    e.g.   real – really; careful – carefully

c   If an adjective ends in *-le*, we drop the *-e* and just add *-y*.
    e.g.   incredible – incredibly; terrible – terribly; gentle – gently;
        idle – idly

d   If an adjective ends in *-e* (apart from *-le*), we usually keep the *-e*.
    e.g.   safe – safely; nice – nicely; extreme – extremely

     Exceptions: true – truly; due – duly; whole – wholly

e   If an adjective ends in a consonant + *-y*, we drop the *-y* and add
    -ily.
    e.g.   steady – steadily; lucky – luckily; merry – merrily;
        temporary – temporarily; easy – easily; heavy – heavily;
        happy – happily; ready – readily

     Exceptions: shy – shyly; sly – slyly; dry – dryly (or drily)

f   If an adjective ends in *-ic*, we add *-ally*.
    e.g.   automatic – automatically; basic – basically

     Exception: public – publicly

Note: Many adverbs end in *-ly* (e.g. greatly, really) but some do
not (e.g. so, too, quite).

Read the letter below. Turn each adjective in brackets into an adverb.

Dear Mr Smithson,

Please accept my apologies for the unpardonable delay in answering your letter of 16 May. *(Unfortunate)*, my secretary was off sick for nearly two months and, most *(regrettable)*, her temporary replacement proved to be *(extreme)* unreliable. In fact, she was *(utter)* incompetent.

It was not until my regular secretary returned that your letter was discovered – together with thirty others – locked away in a drawer. Such things do *(occasional)* occur even in the most efficient of companies, and once again I wish to say how *(true)* sorry I am.

In your letter you ask for details of our course on 'How to become a millionaire'. Please send me £50 *(immediate)* and I shall *(glad)* provide you with your first lesson.

In the meantime, I *(humble)* beg you to reflect on the following testimonial from a client who has *(happy)* parted with £50 in order to enrol on our *(incredible)* successful course for potential millionaires:

'This is *(simple)* the best get-rich-quick scheme on the market. I know that I will *(easy)* get my money back – and more. For example, I was paid £15 to give this testimonial. That shows that this scheme *(real)* does work.' – Sidney, Sussex.

I look forward to receiving your cheque or postal order.

Yours *(sincere)*,

Max Smart

(Max Smart)

(Answers: page 182)

7 Adverbs 3: using adverbs

a We use adverbs with 'active' verbs (= 'doing' words) to show, for example, how something is being done.

   e.g. He drove <u>carelessly</u>. / She sings <u>beautifully</u>.

b An adverb is also used to give extra information about an adjective or another adverb. An adverb can also be an independent phrase commenting on a whole sentence.

   e.g. She is <u>really</u> nice. / She spoke <u>too</u> quickly. / <u>Luckily</u>, nobody was injured.

c We use an <u>adjective</u> – not an adverb – with 'non-active' verbs that describe appearance, a state or condition (= what someone / something is like).

   e.g. That looks interesting. / That smells delicious. / He seems nice.

d We use adjectives instead of adverbs in certain fixed phrases.

   e.g. keep quiet / open wide / hold tight

e The adverbial form of *good* is *well*. Some words (e.g. fast, late, hard) function as adjectives and adverbs.

   e.g. He did well. / He arrived late. / She worked hard.

Look at the words that have been underlined in the sentences below. If the word is written correctly, tick it. If the word is grammatically wrong, correct it.

1   Try to work as <u>fast</u> as you can.

2   Try to work as <u>quick</u> as you can.

3   As the road was slippery, he drove <u>careful</u> and <u>slow</u>.

4   He asked her to keep <u>quiet</u>.

5   He shut the door <u>quiet</u>.

6   She plays football as <u>good</u> as any of the boys in the class.

7   They were supposed to be a <u>strong</u> team, but we beat them <u>easy</u>.

8   She looked rather <u>anxious</u>.

9   She looked <u>anxiously</u> at her brother.

10   She finds it very difficult to write <u>neat</u>.

(Answers: page 182)

8   # American and British spelling

A Where differences exist between American and British spelling, the spelling in American English tends to be simpler.

Note carefully the following:

a   American (*-or*):   **e.g.**   behavior, color, favor, honor, neighbor
     British (*-our*):   **e.g.**   behaviour, colour, favour, honour, neighbour

> *Note:* British English is not consistent and some nouns end in *-or* (e.g. horror, terror).

b   American (*-er*):   **e.g.**   center, fiber, liter, meager, somber, theater
     British (*-re*):   **e.g.**   centre, fibre, litre, meagre, sombre, theatre

c   American (*-se*):   **e.g.**   defense, license (noun), offense
     British (*-ce*):   **e.g.**   defence, licence (noun), offence, practice (noun)
     American (*-ce*):   **e.g.**   practice (verb, noun)
     British (*-se*):   **e.g.**   practise (verb)

> *Note:* With certain words in British English, we indicate the noun form with a *c* and the verb form with an *s*.
> e.g.   to practise – a lot of practice; to advise – a piece of advice; to devise – a device; to license – a licence

d   American: **e.g.**   a computer program, a TV program
     British: **e.g.**   a computer program, a TV / theatre / social programme

e   American: **e.g.**   ax, catalog, dialog
     British: **e.g.**   axe, catalogue, dialogue

f American (*-ize*): e.g. apologize, modernize, realize
British (*-ize / ise*): e.g. apologize | apologise, modernize |
modernise, realize | realise

> *Note:* Except for a few words like *advertise, advise, devise,*
> *supervise* and *surprise*, it is entirely up to you whether to
> use *-ize* or *-ise*. Although dictionaries tend to favour *-ize*, it
> is more practical to use the *-ise* form. Just over a hundred
> years ago, the *-ize* form was prevalent in British English.
> Nowadays, however, the simpler *-ise* form is equally popular.

B In American English, certain words and combinations of letters are
spelt the way they are pronounced. Those same words and
combinations of letters are spelt slightly differently in British
English.

Note carefully the following:

a In each of the following pairs, the first word is British and the
second word is American:
e.g. cheque – check; cosy – cozy; draught – draft; grey – gray;
plough – plow; jewellery – jewelry; mould – mold;
moustache – mustache; pyjamas – pajamas; sceptical –
skeptical; through – thru; tyre – tire

b American (*-e*):   e.g. anesthetic, archeology, encyclopedia,
hemorrhage
British (*-ae*):   e.g. anaesthetic, archaeology, encyclopaedia,
haemorrhage

> *Note:* It is also acceptable to write *encyclopedia* in British
> English.

c American (*-yze*): e.g. analyze, paralyze
British (*-yse*): e.g. analyse, paralyse

d American (*-ll*): e.g. appall, enroll, installment, skillful
British (*-l*):   e.g. appal, enrol, instalment, skilful

e American (*-l*):   e.g. dialed, equaled, instal, marvelous,
traveled, traveler, woolen
British (*-ll*):   e.g. dialled, equalled, install, marvellous,
travelled, traveller, woollen

> *Note:* Technically, *to install* is like *to forestall* and should end in *-ll*, but in practice it is often spelt with one *l* (*to instal*) in British English. Either form is acceptable.

TASK

Underline and change any examples of American spelling in the sentences below. Tick any sentence which is acceptable in British English.

1 She was upset by her neighbor's behavior.

2 Blue is her favorite color.

3 He used his driving license as a means of identification.

4 As it was his first offense, he was let off with a warning.

5 There's an interesting program on TV tonight.

6 She looked at him in horror.

7 If you want to do that particular course, you need to enroll before 10 September.

8 She apologised when she realized her mistake.

(Answers: page 183)

9 Apostrophes 1: to show omission

When we are speaking quickly, we often combine two words to form one word. When we are writing in an informal, relaxed manner, we can do the same with written English.

a To show that two words have been combined into one, we use an apostrophe ('). The apostrophe replaces one letter or more.

  e.g. I'm = I am; he'll = he will; she'd = she had or she would;
       he wasn't = he was not; I don't = I do not;
       we didn't = we did not

Remember to place the apostrophe exactly where the missing letter(s) should be.

   ✗ | She could'nt find her glasses.

   ✓ | She couldn't find her glasses.

   ✗ | I have'nt finished yet.

   ✓ | I haven't finished yet.

b Note the following:

  e.g. It's green.   = It <u>is</u> green.
       It's got three wheels. = It <u>has</u> got three wheels.
       Let's go!   = Let <u>us</u> go!

Look carefully at the writing on the postcard below. Some of the words need an apostrophe ('). Underline them and add the apostrophes.

Dear Mark, Martha, Michelle and Dominic,

Hi! How is your holiday? Were having lots of fun, and doing lots of walking here in Wales. The weathers been lovely, but its beginning to cloud over now. Hope youre enjoying the summer.

Lots of love,

Anna, Frances, Pip and Tom.

(Answers: page 183)

10 Apostrophes 2: to show possession

a We use the apostrophe + -s to show a 'possessive' or 'belonging' relationship between two nouns.
   e.g. my sister's bedroom
       my brother's friend

b It is sometimes possible to leave out the second noun in a 'possessive' phrase.
   e.g. to go to the doctor's (= to go to the doctor's surgery)
       at the butcher's (= at the butcher's shop)
       at my gran's (= at my grandmother's house)

c We may leave out the second noun in order to avoid unnecessary repetition.
   e.g. Susan's hair is longer than Ann's. (= Ann's hair)
       Paula's story is more interesting than Fiona's. (= Fiona's story)

d If the first noun in a possessive relationship already has an -s, we simply add an apostrophe to show that it is a plural noun.
   e.g. my friend's money (= the money belonging to a friend of mine)
       my friends' money (= the money belonging to some friends of mine)
   similarly,
       the boy's pyjamas (We are talking about one boy.)
       the boys' pyjamas (We are talking about more than one boy.)

e If a plural noun does not end in -s (e.g. women, men, children, people), we treat it like a normal noun and add an apostrophe +-s.
   e.g. The men's cloakroom / The children's toys /
       Women's clothes tend to be more expensive than men's.

f If a singular noun (usually the name of a person) ends in *-s*, you can add either *-'s* or just an apostrophe.

Doris's hat / Doris' hat

Mr Jones's car / Mr Jones' car

For longer words, it is best to use an apostrophe after the *-s*.
e.g. Mr Jenkins is married. / Mr Jenkins' children are married.

g We use the apostrophe in phrases showing duration of time.
e.g. a fortnight's holiday; in a year's time; in two months' time

> *Note:* We do not use the apostrophe in time phrases if the last word is an adjective.
> **e.g.** He is six years old. / She is seven months pregnant.

h The apostrophe is used to form the plurals of letters and numbers.
e.g. Dot the i's and cross the t's.
Three 3's are nine.

For numbers over nine, it is up to you whether to use an apostrophe or not.
e.g. in the 1930s / in the 1930's

> *Note:* We dot the i's simply to avoid confusion, as without the apostrophe *i's* could be read as *is*.

i Some words do not require an apostrophe to show that they are 'possessive'. Be particularly careful with the spelling of possessive <u>adjectives</u> (= *whose, my, your, his, her, its, our, their*) and possessive <u>pronouns</u> (= *mine, yours, his, hers, ours, theirs*).

j Certain words sound alike and are often confused. Note carefully the following:

- *whose / who's*
  Whose car is it? = Who does this car belong to? (possessive)
  Who's in the car? = Who is in the car?
  Who's taken my car? = Who has taken my car?

- *your | you're*
  Is this your coat?   = Does this coat belong to you? (possessive)
  You're wearing my coat.   = You are wearing my coat.

- *there | their | they're*
  There it is! (*There* is the opposite of *here*.)

  It's their ball.   = The ball belongs to them. (possessive)
  They're here.   = They are here.

- *there's | theirs*
  There's something wrong. = There is something wrong.
  It's not theirs.   = It does not belong to them. (possessive)

- *it's | its*
  It's green.   = It is green.
  It's been raining.   = It has been raining.

  The school wants to change its image. (*its* = possessive; the image belongs to the school)

k In formal English, we can use *one* to mean *you* (in general). To make *one* possessive, we add apostrophe +-*s*.
  e.g. One shouldn't waste one's time. = You shouldn't waste your time.

TASK

I Can you spot the mistakes? In each of the sentences below, there is one word that should not have an apostrophe. Underline and correct it.

1 That bag isn't your's! It's my brother's.

2 Here's your luggage. Where's our's?

3 This isn't Yumiko's coat. Her's is brown, but this one's blue.

4 That's not our ball. It's their's.

II Read the following joke and put in the missing apostrophes.

A man went for a brain transplant and was offered the choice of two brains – an architects for £100 and a politicians for £10,000.

"Does that mean that the politicians brain is much better than the architects?" asked the man.

"Not exactly," replied the brain transplant salesman. "Its just that the politicians brain has never been used."

(Answers: page 183)

11 *as* and *like*

In spoken English we tend to use *as* and *like* rather loosely. In informal speech we often use *like* in preference to *as*. In written English, however, we should show that we are aware of the rules that govern the standard use of these two words.

a When choosing between *as* and *like*, it is important to remember that we do not use *like* before a clause (= subject + verb) in standard written English.

> **✗** Like I said last week, I won't be able to attend the next meeting.

> **✓** As I said last week, I won't be able to attend the next meeting.

b When talking about the similarity between people, things and actions, we use either *as* or *like*.

- *Like* is used before a noun or pronoun.
  e.g. He works too hard, (just) like his father. / She swims like a fish.

- *As* is used before a clause or a preposition.
  e.g. He works too hard, (just) as his father did. / In Central America, as in most parts of South America, Spanish is the official language.

c When defining the function, purpose, occupation or role of a person or thing, we use *as* + noun.
  e.g. She managed to get a job as a teacher.

d In situations where we want to say what something <u>seems</u> like, we use *like* + noun and *as if* (or *as though*) + clause.
  e.g. Stop acting like a fool. / She looked as if she had been crying.

e Certain verbs (e.g. describe, regard) automatically take *as*.
e.g. I regard her as my best friend.

With other verbs, the use of *as* or *like* will depend on exactly what you want to say.

e.g. He uses the family home like a hotel. (= He treats the family home as if it were a hotel.) / He wants to use the family home as a hotel. (= He wants to turn the family home into a hotel.)

f We also use *as* with expressions of certainty and agreement.
e.g. As you know, we ... / As we agreed last week, we ...

TASK

Fill in each gap below with *as*, *as if* or *like*.

1 Do _____ you are told!

2 He is _____ his father in many ways.

3 It looks _____ rain.

4 It looks _____ it is going to rain.

5 Please stop treating me _____ I were a five-year-old!

6 Would you stop treating me _____ a five-year-old!

7 She is acting _____ my guardian until my parents return.

8 When in Rome, do _____ the Romans do.

9 You look _____ you have been crying.

10 _____ I said in my letter, I can't help you.

(Answers: page 183)

12 Capital letters

We use capital letters at the beginning of the following kinds of words:

a the names of days, months of the year and festivals
   e.g. Monday / July / Diwali / Christmas

b the names of people, places, countries and organisations
   e.g. Peter / Paris / France / the United Nations

c the names of rivers, oceans and mountains
   e.g. the (River) Nile / the Pacific Ocean / Mount Everest

d titles (when they are used with a name)
   e.g. Doctor Jekyll and Mr Hyde / Queen Elizabeth / Captain Hook

e abbreviation of titles
   e.g. Dr Goodfellow / Mr Christian

   Be careful not to confuse normal *common* nouns with *proper*
   nouns (which begin with a capital letter). The particular name of a
   person, place or institution is classed as a *proper* noun. A *common*
   noun is a normal noun being used in a general sense.
   e.g. He is a doctor. He works in a hospital.

   Here are the same nouns being used as proper nouns:
   e.g. Do you know *Dr Smith*? He works at St George's *Hospital*.

f the main words of the title of a book or film
   e.g. James and the Giant Peach / Treasure Island /
          Independence Day / Jurassic Park

g the names of languages, nationality and school subjects
   e.g. French / Irish / Mathematics

h the pronoun 'I'
   e.g. I told them I wasn't interested.

i at the beginning of a sentence
   e.g. The tallest living animal is the giraffe. It lives in Africa.

j at the beginning of direct speech

   e.g. He said, "Come along, please."

> *Note:* Capitals are not necessary for the seasons of the year.
> e.g. in summer, in autumn, in winter, in spring

TASK

I In the joke below, underline and change any word that should start with a capital letter.

an englishman, a scotsman and a welshman were stranded on a small island in the atlantic ocean. one day they found a magic lamp. when they rubbed it, a genie appeared and granted each of them one wish.

"i'd like to be back in birmingham," said the englishman. puff! he disappeared.

"i'd like to be back in glasgow," said the scotsman. puff! he disappeared.

"gosh," said the welshman, "i'm very lonely here on my own. i wish my friends were back again." puff! puff!

II Read the following advertisement for a pen friend. Begin some of the words with a capital letter.

my name is thomas smythe and i come from sheffield. i will be eleven next april. i don't have any brothers or sisters, but i've got a dog called bono.
i speak a little bit of french and i know a few words of spanish (i've been to spain twice).
my favourite subject at school is english and my favourite pop group is 'slick girls'.
i love playing football and i support sheffield united. my ambition is to play for england.

(Answers: page 183)

13 Colons (:)

a   You should not link two separate sentences with a comma. It is possible, however, to join two separate sentences with a colon. The colon is a 'linking' punctuation mark that allows you to proceed with some kind of summary, illustration or direct explanation of what has just been stated. If you are unsure whether to use a colon or not, it might help you to think of the colon as an equals sign (=).

   e.g.   Lions are very lazy animals: they sleep for most of the day and hunt at night.
          I don't like Mark: he's so selfish.

b   A colon is also used to introduce an example, a quotation or a list of items.

   e.g.   In his pocket they found the following items: a pistol, a knife and a passport.
          Our teacher always uses the same proverb in class: 'more haste, less speed'.

c   A colon is also used to introduce a direct explanation of what has just been stated.

   e.g.   The choice is clear: we either do as he says or we go to the police.

d   A colon may be used instead of a comma to introduce direct speech.

   e.g.   While they were waiting for the police to arrive, he whispered to her: "Don't mention the money." She nodded and said: "Don't worry, I won't say anything."

e   Unless direct speech is involved, the first word after a colon does not usually start with a capital letter. In American English, however, the first word after a colon usually begins with a capital letter.

I By taking out two words and using a colon, make the two sentences below into one sentence.

The rainbow has seven colours. They are red, orange, yellow, green, blue, indigo and violet.

II By using a colon, reduce the pieces of writing below from three sentences to two.

1 The dodo was a big flightless bird. There are no dodos left alive today. They are extinct.

2 There is not much difference between rabbits and hares. They both have long ears and long back legs. Hares are slightly larger and move by jumping, whereas rabbits move by running.

(Answers: page 184)

14 Commas 1: when to pause

a   General use of the comma:

When we speak, we pause naturally at certain places. In the same way, a comma indicates a very brief pause within a sentence.
e.g.   By the way, have you seen Michael?
Excuse me, is this the right way to the station?

Sentences can sound different depending on the use of a comma.
Read aloud the two sentences below:
Of course I'll help you.
Of course, you don't have to go if you don't want to.

b   In the same way that a full stop prevents one sentence from running into another, so too a comma prevents words within a sentence from running into each other.

c   We use a comma between items or names in a list. We do not usually place a comma before the final *and / or* in a list of items or names.
e.g.   You can have an apple, a banana or a pear.
I went on a picnic with Christopher, Mark, Nick and Sarah.

d   We also use commas to separate a series of verbs that have the same subject.
e.g.   He walked into the room, said 'hello', poured himself a drink and sat down.

e   Words that form part of an introduction to the main message of the sentence are usually marked off by a comma.
e.g.   Not feeling well, she decided to stay at home.
Actually, I'm not late!

f   If we begin a sentence with such words as *although, despite, if, when, after, before, as soon as, just as, as, while, etc.*, we should use a comma before beginning the main part of the sentence.
e.g.   <u>Despite</u> the weather, we had a great time.
<u>If</u> it rains, we will watch a video.

On the other hand, a comma is usually quite unnecessary if the main part of the sentence comes first.

e.g. We had a great time <u>despite</u> the weather.

We'll watch a video <u>if</u> it rains.

g When we use *so* to join two parts of a sentence, we usually put a comma before it.

e.g. We arrived early, so we had to wait.

We were late, so we missed the train.

> *Note:* In the examples above, *so* means 'and for that reason'.

TASK

Here are three jokes. Read them aloud. Add commas where necessary.

1 Gary: Have you been invited to Rashid's party?
   Mike: Yes, but I can't go.
   Gary: Why not?
   Mike: The invitation says 4 to 7, and I am eight.

2 "Dad, will you do my homework for me?"
   "No, it wouldn't be right."
   "Well, at least you can try."

3 Traveller: Excuse me, do you have a room for tonight?
   Hotel proprietor: Certainly sir. It'll be £50 a night, or I can let you have a room for only £10, if you make your own bed.
   Traveller: I'll take the £10 room.
   Hotel proprietor: Right! I'll just go and fetch, the wood, the hammer, and the nails for the bed.

(Answers: page 184)

15   Commas 2: how to pause

a   The golden rule when using the comma is not to overuse it. If in doubt, omit it.

b   Never use a comma to <u>join</u> two complete sentences.

> [✗] I liked the book, it was really exciting.

> [✓] I liked the book. It was really exciting.

> [✓] I liked the book because it was really exciting.

c   We should mark off any subsidiary phrase, introductory word(s) or emphatic remark at the beginning of a sentence with a comma.
   e.g. According to the doctors, there is little hope.
       Incidentally, when will the report be ready?
       Lord, hear our prayer.

d   Generally speaking, it is best to place a comma after an adverb or adverbial phrase at the beginning of a sentence.
   e.g. Sadly, the dog died afterwards.
       Miraculously, he survived the crash.
       All of a sudden, she burst into tears.

On the other hand, the structure / flow of a sentence may sometimes make it unnecessary or awkward to include a comma after an adverb or adverbial phrase.
   e.g. Suddenly it began to pour down with rain and, not having an umbrella, I got completely soaked.

e   Subordinate clauses and adjectival phrases that follow a main clause may also be marked off by a comma.
   e.g. The waiter spilt some wine on my suit, completely ruining it.
       I went to bed, tired but happy.
       Although the meeting lasted all day, no decisions were reached.

f   When we join two independent clauses with a conjunction (e.g. and, but, or), we have the option of placing a comma before the conjunction if we feel it is necessary.
   e.g. I wanted to book our tickets in advance, but the ticket-office was closed for the weekend.

g   With direct speech, we use the comma in the following way:
e.g.   He said, "Ah, yes, Mr Bond. Please come in."
"Please come in," he said. "I shall be with you in a moment."
"I'm not sure," he said, "but I think it is on Wednesday."

h   When using commas, you need to decide whether to use one
comma (to mark off a division in a sentence) or two commas
(to enclose an interruption within a sentence).
e.g.   During most of the Middle Ages, few people were able to read
or write. / During most of the Middle Ages, few people,
including kings and emperors, were able to read or write.

i   There are times when the grammar of a sentence demands the
'correct' use of the comma. More often than not, however, the use
of the comma is a matter of personal preference and style.

TASK

Supply commas where appropriate in the passages below.

1 The lawyer and the oyster

As two men were walking along the seashore they found an
oyster and began to quarrel about it.
"I saw it first" said one of the men "so it belongs to me."
"I picked it up" said the other "so I have a right to keep it."
As they were quarrelling a lawyer came by and they asked him
to decide for them in the matter.
The lawyer agreed to do so but before he would give his
opinion he required the two men to give him their assurance
that they would agree to whatever he decided.
Then the lawyer said "It seems to me that you both have a
claim to the oyster; so I will divide it between you and you will
then be perfectly satisfied."
Opening the oyster he quickly ate it and very gravely handed
an empty shell to each of the men.
"But you have eaten the oyster!" cried the men.
"Ah that was my fee for deciding the case!" said the lawyer.
"But I have divided all that remains in a perfectly fair and just
manner."
That is what happens when two quarrelsome persons go to law
about something that they cannot agree upon.

2 Heroism at sea

When the steamship *Stella* left Southampton on the afternoon before Good Friday in the year 1899 she was bound for the Channel Islands with nearly two hundred passengers on board.

Not long after the ship had started her voyage the sea became covered with fog. The captain hoped it would lift and kept the ship at full speed. But the fog grew thicker and the *Stella* crashed on some rocks. The lifeboats were lowered and the passengers behaved as bravely as men and women can in a crisis.

But the name of one woman will always be remembered when people think of the sinking of the *Stella*. Mrs Mary Rogers the stewardess comforted the women and gave each of them a life-belt fastening it with her own hands. She led them to the side of the sinking ship where the boats were being lowered. At the last moment it was found that one woman had no life-belt. Instantly the stewardess took off her own belt and gave it up and the woman was lifted safely into the boat. The sailors called to the stewardess to jump in but the boat was full.

"No no!" she said. "There is no room. One more and the boat will sink."

The ship sank into the sea and Mary Rogers looked on the world for the last time.

"Goodbye goodbye!" she cried and then: "Lord take me!"

Within a minute the *Stella* was gone and with her the brave stewardess.

(Answers: page 184)

16 Commas 3: the comma and relative clauses

A *relative clause* is a subordinate clause which gives more information about someone or something mentioned in the main clause. Relative clauses usually begin with a relative pronoun (e.g. that, which, who, whom, whose) (see Unit 41). When considering the use of the comma with relative clauses, we need to bear in mind that there are two kinds of relative clauses: *defining* and *non-defining*.

a   A *defining* relative clause is one that identifies the person or thing being spoken about. Since this information is essential to the meaning of a sentence, no commas are used.

e.g.   An architect is a person *who designs houses.*
A burglar is someone *who breaks into a house to steal things.*
The only mammal *that flies* is the bat.

If we took out the defining relative clauses, the sentences would clearly be incomplete.

b   A *non-defining* relative clause gives further information about someone or something. We should think of a non-defining clause as an additional comment. We separate an additional comment from a main clause by means of the comma.

e.g.   I am reading a book on graphology, *which is the study of handwriting.*
The most important vegetable in the world is the tomato, *which is used in more than 100 countries.*

If we took out the non-defining relative clause, the sentences would still make perfect sense.

c   Be careful when using the comma with a relative clause. When <u>enclosing</u> a relative clause within a main clause, make sure that you use two commas. Use one comma when the relative clause follows on from the main clause.

e.g.   The whale shark, which may grow to be forty-five feet long and weigh fifty tons, is harmless. It eats very small animals, which it strains from the sea water.

Supply commas where necessary in the sentences below. Tick any sentence that does not require commas.

1 'An actor is a sculptor who carves in snow.'
(Lawrence Barrett)

2 'Man is the only animal that blushes. Or needs to.' (Mark Twain)

3 'That which is striking and beautiful is not always good; but that which is good is always beautiful.' (Ninon de l'Enclos)

4 Henry VI who was only eight months old when he came to the throne in 1422 was England's youngest king.

5 The only British Prime Minister to have been assassinated was Spencer Perceval (1762–1812) who was shot dead when entering the lobby of the House of Commons.

6 The first woman in space was Valentina Tereshkova of the former Soviet Union who orbited the Earth in June 1963.

7 Louis Pasteur whose work on wine, vinegar and beer led to pasteurisation had an obsessive fear of dirt and infection. He would never shake hands with anybody.

8 The German physicist Wilhelm Konrad Roentgen who discovered X-rays and initiated a scientific revolution in doing so refused to apply for any patents in connection with the discovery or to make any financial gains out of it. He died in poverty.

9 The Dutch painter Van Meegeren who lived from 1899 to 1947 pulled off some of the most brilliant forgeries in art history.

10 'Anthony Edwards has become television's highest-paid actor in a deal which ties him to the hospital drama *ER* for the next four years.

Edwards who plays Dr Mark Greene has signed a £21 million contract: equivalent to almost £250,000 an episode.

George Clooney who previously had the largest salary is leaving the series early next year.'

(Answers: page 185)

17 Common spelling errors

Certain words cause more spelling problems than others. You should get into the habit of grouping the most troublesome ones together – and then learn them by heart. Note carefully the word groups below:

a *ie/ei*
- The basic rule is '*i* before *e* except after *c*' when the sound is *ee*, as in *cheese*.
  e.g. Group 1: believe, relief, chief, brief, fierce, piece
  Group 2: conceited, receive, receipt, deceive, ceiling

  There are, however, exceptions to the rule.
  e.g. seize, Neil, Sheila, Keith, protein, weird

- We write *ei* when the sound is *ay*, as in *play*.
  e.g. neighbour, rein, reign, vein, weigh, eight

- We write *ie* after *c* or *t* when the sound is *sh*.
  e.g. ancient, species, efficient, sufficient, patient

- When *i* and *e* are separate sounds, the spelling is straightforward.
  e.g. diet, drier, science

- Finally, some words we simply have to learn by heart.
  e.g. foreign, leisure, neither

b Words with tricky vowel sounds:
e.g. definite, responsible, medicine, separate, village, cabbage, message, sausage, foliage, luggage, library, temporary, burglar, television, millionaire

c Difficult adverbs:
e.g. immediately, deliberately, unfortunately, desperately, particularly

d Use of double consonants:

- *app-*
  e.g. apple, appetite, appoint(ment), apply, application, approve

- *opp-*
  e.g. opposite, opportunity, opponent

- *acc-*
  e.g. accompany, accept, access, accident, accommodation

- *occ-*
  e.g. occasion, occur, occupy

- *-rr-*
  e.g. carrot, embarrassed, parrot

e One *c* or two?
Group 1: succeed, success, successful
Group 2: necessary, recommend

f *ex-*
e.g. except, exception, excited, exhausted

g Double trouble (= words that are a real headache!)
e.g. address, bizarre, blizzard, collision, difficulty, exaggerate,
intelligent, parallel, professional, scissors, toffee

h Silent letters
The sound of a word in English does not necessarily indicate how
the word will be spelt. This is particularly true of words with silent
letters (= letters that are not pronounced). It is important that you
should be aware of the most common words with silent letters.

Word	Silent letter
• carriage, marriage	a
• plumber, doubt, debt, numb	b
• scientist, conscious, acquire, acquaint	c
• judge, hedge, adjust, adjourn	d
• shone, axe, engine	e
• gnaw, campaign	g
• weight, height, taught	gh
• character, ache, honour, rhyme	h

- knot, knuckle   k
- could, would, salmon, calm, half, calf   l
- autumn, solemn, government, environment   n
- pneumonia, psychology, receipt   p
- island, isle   s
- castle, listen, fetch, catch   t
- guard, guarantee   u
- write, wrong, sword, answer   w

TASK

I Read the following jokes and underline the correct alternative in brackets.

1 My (niece / neice), (Shiela / Sheila) has a very sweet tooth. One day she entered a restaurant and ordered a whole chocolate cake for lunch. "Shall I cut it into four (pieces / peices) or eight?" asked the waitress.
"Four," she said. "I'm on a (diet / deit)."

2 The bats were hanging upside down from the (ceiling / cieling) of a cave. All except one, who was hanging with his head upwards.
"That's a bit (wierd / weird), isn't it?" whispered one bat to another. "What's the matter with your (freind / friend)?"
"Be (quiet / queit)!" whispered the other bat. "He's taken up yoga."

II How many spelling mistakes can you find in the jokes below? Correct the mistakes.

1 Hotel manager: Some of our guests seem to regard our cutlary as a form of medecine.
   Diner: How do you mean?
   Hotel manager: To be taken after meals.

2 Ron: What's your New Year's resolution?
   Bert: To be much less concieted.
   Ron: Won't that be dificult to maintain for a year?
   Bert: Not for someone as clever and inteligent as me.

(Answers: page 186)

18 Comparisons: comparatives and superlatives

a When we say *smaller*, we are using the <u>comparative</u> form of *small*. When we say *smallest*, we are using the <u>superlative</u> form of *small*.

b We use the comparative form of a word to make a comparison <u>between one</u> person / group / item / situation <u>and another</u> person / group / item / situation.
  e.g. She is taller than her brother. / He took the bigger piece. / It will be quicker by train than by bus.

c We normally use *than* to join the two halves of a comparison. Note, however, that we say that one person / item is *different from* another person / item.

d We use *fewer* – not *less* – with plural nouns.
  e.g. There are fewer people here today than there were yesterday.

e We use *less* with singular nouns.
  e.g. A shower provides less water than a bath.

f We use the superlative form of a word when we wish to select <u>one</u> person / item <u>from</u> a group.
  e.g. She is the tallest in the class. / He is the eldest of the three.

(see also Unit 4 'd')

g Forming comparatives and superlatives

It is important not to confuse adjectives and adverbs when making comparisons.

- For most adverbs (ending in *-ly*), we use *more* (= comparative) and *most* (= superlative).
  e.g. He asked her to drive more carefully.
  The longest we can stay is a week.
  Please speak more slowly.

- For one-syllable adjectives, add *-er* or *-est.*

  (see also Unit 4)

  e.g. big – bigger – biggest; clean – cleaner – cleanest

- For adjectives of two syllables ending in consonant *+-y*, drop the *-y* and add *-ier* or *-iest.*

  e.g. pretty – prettier – prettiest; easy – easier – easiest

- For certain two-syllable adjectives (e.g. narrow, simple, common, clever), we can use *-er* and *-est.*

  e.g. simple – simpler – simplest

- For all other long-sounding adjectives of two syllables or more, we use *more* and *most.*

  e.g. intelligent – more intelligent – most intelligent

- Certain adverbs and adjectives share the same comparative and superlative form.

  e.g. good / well – better – best; bad / badly – worse – worst; fast – faster – fastest; early – earlier – earliest; soon – sooner – soonest; late – later – latest; hard – harder – hardest

---

Note: In American English *different than* is possible. *Different to* is not used.

TASK

I   Look at the pairs of sentences below. In each case, one of the sentences has a grammatical error. The other sentence is grammatically correct. Find the error and correct it.

1 a He is the most cleverest person I have ever met.
   b She is cleverer than you think.

2 a My cold is getting worse.
   b Honestly, it was the worse day of my life.

3 a Ivan is undoubtedly the best player in the team.
   b If I have to choose between Ahmed and Tariq, I think Ahmed is the best player.

4 a The patient recovered quicker than expected.
   b The patient's recovery was quicker than expected.

5 a You should eat less chocolate and fewer biscuits.

  b There have been far less burglaries in this area this year than there were last year.

6 a They are as different as chalk from cheese.

  b The film is completely different than the book.

II Complete the sentences below with the correct alternative given in italics.

neater / more neatly

  1 The teacher asked her to write _____ .

  2 Her handwriting is _____ than mine.

less / fewer

  3 His dentist told him to eat _____ sweets in future.

  4 In the examination, he should have spent _____ time on Section A.

  5 There are _____ candidates for the examination this year.

better / best

  6 Of the two, Elena is the _____ linguist.

  7 Elena is the _____ linguist the school has ever produced.

  8 It was a close match, but there is no doubt that the _____ team won.

worse / worst

  9 His bark is _____ than his bite.

  10 I reckon I am _____ off than before.

  11 Marrying him was the _____ thing she could possibly have done.

(Answers: page 186)

19 # Concord: subject-verb agreement

a Concord, or agreement, follows a set of simple rules.

Singular subjects go with singular verb phrases.

Plural subjects go with plural verb phrases.
e.g. He walks to work every day. / They walk to work every day.

b When we are talking about the present, we add -*s* to a verb if one person or thing (he / she / it) is performing the action or being described by the verb.

1 When adding -*s* to a verb, we apply the following rules:

- Normally, we add just -*s*.
  e.g. come – she comes; laugh – he laughs; work – it works

- If there is a vowel in front of -*y*, the -*y* does not change when we add -*s*.
  e.g. say – she says; play – he plays; stay – it stays

- If there is a consonant in front of -*y*, the ending becomes -*ies* when we add -*s*.
  e.g. try – she tries; study – he studies; worry – he worries

- We add -*es* to verbs ending in -*o*, -*ss*, -*ch*, -*sh* and -*x*. We do this in order to make it easier to pronounce the words.
  e.g. go – he goes; miss – she misses; watch – he watches;
    wash – it washes; fix – she fixes

2 The verbs *be* and *have* are irregular verbs and we say:
e.g. he / she / it *is*
    he / she / it *has*

(see Unit 30)

c   We normally use a singular verb with these kinds of words:
    e.g. it, one (of), each (of), every, nobody, no one, everybody,
        everyone, anybody, anyone, neither (of), either (of), furniture,
        information, rubbish, luggage, advice, Mathematics, Physics,
        athletics, gymnastics, measles, news

d   We use a singular verb when describing an amount or quantity.
    e.g. Six months is a long time to be off school.
        Five thousand dollars is a lot of money.

e   We use a singular verb with *neither ... nor / either ... or* if there are
    just two people or things involved. If one of the nouns is plural,
    then the verb agrees with the nearer noun.
    e.g. Neither Mary nor James <u>was</u> invited to the party.
        Neither Mary nor her friends <u>were</u> invited to the party.
        Neither the twins nor John <u>was</u> invited to the party.

f   We can use either a singular verb or a plural verb for many 'group'
    nouns (e.g. family, team, class, club, public, government,
    committee, school, company, firm, staff, crew, orchestra, choir).

    Your choice of verb will depend on whether you are viewing the
    group as a whole (= as a single unit) or as a number of individuals
    in a group. The important point is to be consistent with
    accompanying words such as *it* or *they*.
    e.g. The jury <u>has</u> reached <u>its</u> verdict.
        The jury <u>are</u> still discussing the case. <u>They</u> have been out for
        ten hours.

g   We use a plural verb for the following words:
    e.g. scissors, trousers, police, people

h   We use a plural verb with 'a number of' (= some) and a singular
    verb with '*the* number of'.

i   If *there* + verb introduces a singular noun (on its own, or the first
    of a list), the verb will be singular. If *there* + verb introduces a
    plural noun, the verb will be plural.
    e.g. There is a pen on your desk.
        There's a pen, two rubbers and a pencil on your desk.
        There are two pens, a rubber and a pencil on your desk.

I Read the three passages given below and look at each verb in brackets. Does it need to change in any way? Tick any verb that does not need to be changed. Write out any verb that needs to be changed.

1 Breathing through the lungs

Mammals (have) lungs. When we (breathe) in, air (go) through the nose and mouth and then down a long tube to the lungs. The lungs (be) like spongy bags. Inside the lungs, oxygen (pass) from the air into the blood. The blood (carry) the oxygen to every part, or cell, of the body. The other gases in the air (pass) out of the body when we (breathe) out.

2 The cuckoo

The cuckoo never (make) a nest. She (lay) her eggs in the nests of other birds. The cuckoo always (choose) a nest where the eggs (look) like her own. She (take) one egg from the nest and (leave) her own in its place. Then she (fly) off with the stolen egg.

When the mother bird (return) to the nest, she (have) no idea that there (be) a cuckoo egg in her nest. But as soon as the eggs (hatch), the cuckoo (create) a lot of trouble because of its size and strength and (force) all the other young birds out of the nest. The mother bird then just (feed) and (care) for the young cuckoo.

3 The camel

When a camel (go) on a long journey, it (carry) its food with it. For days before it (start) its journey, a camel (do) nothing but eat and drink. It (eat) so much that a hump of fat (rise) on its back. The camel's body (use) up this fat during the long journey.

II Underline the correct alternative in brackets.

1 A number of students (has / have) been suspended.

2 The number of students attending school (have / has) increased from 500 to 600.

3 One in six people (suffer / suffers) from insomnia.

4 One of the children (have / has) caught malaria.

5 There (were / was) a lot of people at the party.

6 There (is / are) two biscuits left. Do you want one?

7 Most of my luggage (is / are) still missing.

8 The news (was / were) better than expected.

9 The scissors (is / are) on the table.

10 Ten miles (is / are) a long way to walk!

11 Each of my brothers (has / have) his own room.

12 My family (were / was) delighted with their presents.

13 The crew (was / were) tired after their long flight.

14 (Has / Have) everybody left the building?

15 Gymnastics (was / were) my favourite activity at school.

(Answers: page 187)

20 **Dashes (–)**

a The dash is a very versatile punctuation mark. More often than not, a dash can be used in place of a comma, colon or semicolon. It is also a fairly informal punctuation mark, and should not be overused in your writing. As you study the examples below, note that sometimes we need to use a pair of dashes and sometimes a single dash.

b We can use pairs of dashes (instead of commas or brackets) to mark an interruption within a sentence.

e.g. And then Henry – who's as strong as an ox – arrived on the scene, and together we managed to chase the gang away.

c We can use pairs of dashes to emphasise a word or phrase.

e.g. If the human appendix becomes inflamed, it has to be taken out – fast – by what is nowadays a simple operation.

d When adding an explanation or introducing a list, we can use a dash instead of a colon.

e.g. I found the exam extremely difficult – half the questions were impossible to answer!

e   Before an afterthought (in informal English), we use a dash.
   e.g. I sent Henry an invitation – at least, I think I did!

f   To create a dramatic pause, we can use a dash.
   e.g. I looked up – and saw Stella with a gun in her hand.
         I looked up and saw Stella – with a gun in her hand.

TASK

I Insert dashes where appropriate in the sentences below.

1   Bats are not birds they are mammals.

2   He said he would do it and he did!

3   There was only one other customer an untidy, middle-aged man
    with a pair of binoculars slung over his shoulder.

4   And don't forget we leave in an hour.

5   He saw the red light in the middle of the road. It was being
    waved slowly up and down the international signal to stop.

II Insert dashes where appropriate in the sentences below.

1   Vitamin C which is essential for healthy teeth, gums and blood
    vessels can be found in fresh fruit and vegetables.

2   She and Reg had no secrets from each other. Well she laughed
    to herself only one …

3   The speed of sound known as Mach 1, after the Austrian
    physicist and philosopher Ernst Mach is different at different
    heights.

4   The deepest lake in the world it is nearly a mile deep in places
    is Lake Baikal, in Siberia.

5   It wasn't too long ago 1977, to be exact that Cairo, a city of 8
    million people, had only 208,000 telephones and no telephone
    directory.

(Answers: page 187)

21 Direct speech: showing what someone has said

a We use speech marks to show the actual words spoken by someone (= direct speech).

Speech marks may be single ('...') or double ("...").

Any other punctuation mark should go inside the speech marks.
e.g. "How are you?" he said.
"Get out!" he shouted.

b When creating a dialogue, we show that two people are speaking by putting their words on separate lines. Within the speech marks, we use the punctuation marks we would normally use for one sentence or more.
e.g. "I've lost my dog."
"Why don't you put an advertisement in the paper?"
"Don't be silly! My dog can't read."

c Note, however, that a full stop becomes a comma if we add a phrase like *he said*.
e.g. "I've lost my dog," he said.

d If words like *he said* come before the words in speech marks, we punctuate as follows:
e.g. The soldier shouted, "Run for your lives!"
Then he said, "Why don't we try something else?"

e Now look what happens when a phrase like *he said* is sandwiched between two pieces of direct speech:

- "I've lost my dog. What shall I do?" (two separate sentences)
becomes
"I've lost my dog," he said. "What shall I do?"

- "I've lost my dog, but I think I know where it is." (one sentence)
becomes
"I've lost my dog," he said, "but I think I know where it is."

f We mark the beginning of direct speech with a capital letter even though the words may be in the middle of a sentence.

e.g. He said, "We will see you later."

Note: In a normal sentence where there are no speech marks, we never use a comma to separate phrases like *he said* or *she said that* from the words that follow.

e.g. He said he would do it later.

She said that she didn't like it.

TASK

I Correct the jokes below. Use capital letters, speech marks and other punctuation marks where appropriate.

1 my doctor has advised me to give up golf said fred
why asked his friend did he examine your heart
no replied fred but he had a look at my score card

2 two small boys were discussing their future
what are you going to be when you grow up one of them asked
a soldier answered the other
what if you get killed
who would want to kill me
the enemy
the other boy thought it over
okay he said when I grow up, I'll be the enemy

II Two of the four sentences below are wrongly punctuated. Which two?

1 He said, "I'm not feeling well."

2 He said, he was not feeling well.

3 She said, "I'm freezing."

4 She said that, she was freezing.

(Answers: page 187)

22 **Emphatic English**

a If you read poetry, you will have noticed that one way a poet achieves a dramatic effect is by inverting normal word order.

e.g. Stormed at with shot and shell,
Boldly they rode and well,
Into the jaws of Death,
Into the mouth of Hell
Rode the six hundred.
(From *The Charge of the Light Brigade* by Alfred, Lord Tennyson)

b Inversion is not just a device for poets. In normal prose, a number of adverbial words or phrases can be put at the beginning of a sentence for greater emphasis. These adverbial words/phrases include:

under no circumstances, on no account, not only, hardly, scarcely, no sooner, seldom, rarely, by no means, little, never, at no time, nowhere, not until, only, so, such

We use the question form of a verb after such adverbial expressions.

e.g. Little *did he realise* that he was being watched. | Never *have I been* so insulted!

Note: • *Only* must be followed by a clause or phrase for inversion to take place.

• After *only* and *not until*, inversion takes place in the second part of the sentence.

e.g. Not until I got home did I discover that my wallet was missing.
Only after I got home did I discover that my wallet was missing.

---

c As a more emphatic substitute for *although* + clause, we can use the following patterns:

● *Much as* + subject + verb
e.g. Much as I like pizza, I don't want to eat it every day.

- Adjective + *as* + subject + verb

  e.g. Poor as we are, we are by no means unhappy.

> *Note:* • *Much as* is used only with such personal verbs of feelings as *like, dislike, hate, admire, appreciate, (dis)approve, respect, sympathise, enjoy.*
>
> • After an adjective, we can use *though* instead of *as.*
> **e.g.** Brilliant though he is, he can't do simple arithmetic.
>
> • Note the following fixed phrase:
> <u>Try as he might</u>, he could not get the car to start.

TASK

Finish each sentence in such a way that it means exactly the same as the sentence above it.

1 You must not touch those buttons under any circumstances.

   Under _____

2 They did not find out the truth until twenty years later.

   Not until _____

3 It is by no means certain that they will agree to our plan.

   By _____

4 Although I respect Renata very much, I do not think she is the right person for the job.

   Much _____

5 Despite all his efforts, he could not force the door open.

   Try _____

6 I know this may sound strange, but I don't really want to earn a lot of money.

   Strange _____

(Answers: page 188)

23 **Formal English**

a Traditionally, we conjugated the future tense in the following way:
e.g. I *shall*, we *shall*, you will, they will, he / she / it will

In the same way, we conjugated the conditional tense as follows:
e.g. I *should*, we *should*, you would, they would, he / she / it would

Nowadays, *I / we will* and *I / we would* are perfectly acceptable in standard English. The traditional forms of the future and conditional tenses are still used, however, in formal English.

b In the past, we distinguished between *can* and *may*. That distinction is no longer maintained rigidly in modern English. Between equals, it is more common to use *can* than *may* when asking or giving permission. In question form, *may* certainly sounds more polite than *can* – and should be used on formal occasions. In a statement, however, *may* often sounds cold, distant and officious. Official rules and regulations often contain the word *may*.
e.g. Students may not wear sandals on the premises.

c In formal written English, some writers prefer to follow the traditional rule that *who* changes to *whom* when it is the object of a verb.
e.g. 'We always love those who admire us, and we do not always love those whom we admire.' (La Rochefoucauld)

In modern English, it is perfectly acceptable to use *who* instead of *whom* when it is the object of the verb.
e.g. Who did you see?
Whom did you see? (very formal)

d *Whilst* and *amongst* are more formal than *while* and *among*.

e When talking in general, *one* is the formal equivalent of *you*. *One* can also be used in place of *I*.
e.g. One has certain obligations to one's friends.

f Note the following formal patterns:
- It is vital / essential that something (should) be done.
- We propose / suggest that something (should) be done.

g Conditional statements can be made more formal in the following ways:
- If I were rich… = Were I rich…

- If that were to happen… = Were that to happen…
- If he should need… = Should he need…
- If I had realised… = Had I realised…

TASK

Without changing its meaning, replace each underlined word with a more formal word.

1 I <u>would</u> like to take this opportunity to thank you for all your hard work.

2 You have raised an interesting point and I <u>will</u> certainly give it some thought.

3 "<u>Can</u> I leave the table?" the little boy asked politely.

4 I was shocked when Brian, <u>who</u> I had always considered to be my best friend, took Keith's side in the dispute.

5 In business, <u>you</u> should not allow <u>your</u> feelings to affect <u>your</u> judgement.

(Answers: page 188)

24

Greek and Latin roots

a When we use the term *root*, we mean a word or word element from which other words are formed. Many English words take their roots from Greek and Latin words.

  e.g. *auto* (Greek) = self / by oneself; *bio* (Greek) = life; *audio* (Latin) = I hear; *video* (Latin) = I see; *visus* (Latin) = sight

b We can build upon a root word in three ways:
  - We can combine the root word with other root words.
    e.g. biography, autobiography, autograph, videophone

  - We can add a <u>suffix</u> (i.e. an addition placed at the <u>end</u> of the word).
    e.g. audible, audience, audition, visible, vision, phonetic

  - We can add a <u>prefix</u> (i.e. an addition placed at the <u>beginning</u> of the word).
    e.g. inaudible, invisible, revision

Note: Many of our most common prefixes and suffixes are also Greek or Latin in origin.

---

c Recognising the function and meaning of the most common root words, prefixes and suffixes will help you improve your spelling, increase your vocabulary and develop your reading comprehension skills.

d A knowledge of root words is particularly useful when dealing with specialised / academic vocabulary.
  e.g. What is 'polygamy'?
    What is 'monogamy'?
    What is 'bigamy'?

  (clue: *gamy* = marriage; *poly* = many; *mono* = one; *bi* = two)

  <u>Polygamy</u> is the custom of being married to more than one person at the same time. British law only allows <u>monogamy</u> (being married to one person). If you are married and then marry another person, you are committing the crime of <u>bigamy</u> (being married to two people at the same time).

e When looking up the meaning of a difficult word, it is always worth checking what root words are involved.

I The following words in italics are Greek in origin:

tele = far off, at a distance; *phone* = sound; *graph* = visual symbol (picture or written); *scope* = look at, observe; *micro* = very small

How many English words can you make from these Greek root words by combining one with another?

II In Latin, the past participle of the verb *scribere* (= to write) is *scriptus* (= written). The Latin word for 'hand' is *manus*.

1 Which English word is derived from the combination of *scriptus* and *manus*?

_____

2 What word do we use when we refer to 'cosmetic hand-care'?

_____

3 Which adjective do we use when we refer to 'unskilled' labour?

_____

4 What word do we use when we refer to the sacred writings of a religion?

_____

5 In what contexts do we use the word 'script' in English?

_____

III The root word *cide* means 'killer / killing'. Complete the definitions (1–5) by selecting from the words given. You will not need to use all the words.

| suicide | homicide | herbicide | pesticide | fratricide |
| genocide | matricide | patricide | infanticide | |

1 _____ : the extermination of a whole race or nation

2 _____ : the crime of killing one's father

3 _____ : the act of killing oneself

4 _____ : murder (the killing of another human being)

5 _____ : a chemical used by farmers and gardeners to destroy weeds

(Answers: page 188)

25 Homophones: words that sound alike

a   Words that sound the same are known as *homophones* (from Greek for 'same sound'). The spelling of these words depends on the context in which they are found. In other words, never rely just on the sound of a word when checking your spelling. For example, *great* and *grate* have the same pronunciation, and this causes problems with the word *grateful* (which students often misspell as *greatful*). When in doubt, consult a dictionary.

b   There are five problem areas that you should be aware of when checking your spelling:

● Be careful not to confuse the <u>possessive</u> form of a word with other forms.

   e.g.   <u>its</u> price / it's expensive;
   <u>their</u> car / up there / they're late;
   it is <u>theirs</u> / there's no need

● Be careful with words that have silent letters.
   e.g.   would, write, whole, knight, whine, answer, sword
   (see also Unit 17 'h')

● Be particularly alert to pairs of words where just one letter may completely change the meaning.
   e.g.   canvas (a type of cloth); canvass (seek votes / political support); die / dying (stop living); dye / dyeing (change the colour of things)

● A change of letter may change the grammar of a word.
   e.g.   practice (noun)   licence (noun)   dependant (noun)
   practise (verb)   license (verb)   dependent (adjective)

> *Note:* In American English, however, the distinction between the spelling of nouns / verbs is not so rigid.

● Above all, try not to misspell very basic words.
   e.g.   break / brake   meet / meat   steal / steel
   week / weak   too / two / to   fair / fare

c The existence of homophones in the English language has given rise to a type of humour that is peculiarly British: the pun, or play on words. Here are some examples:

- A teacher saw two boys fighting in the playground.
  "Stop!" he shouted. "You know the rules: no fighting *allowed*!"
  "But, sir, we weren't fighting *aloud*. We were fighting quietly."

- "Waiter, what do you call this?"
  "It's *bean* soup, sir."
  "I don't care what it's *been*. What is it now?"

TASK

I Complete the sentences below with *there*, *their* or *they're*.

1 _____ ready.

2 Who's sitting _____?

3 _____'s a fly in my soup!

4 They forgot _____ books.

5 Have you met my brothers? _____ standing over _____ .

II Use one of the words provided to fill in each gap below.

1 dependant / dependent

She is financially _____ on her parents.

2 counsellor / councillor

A _____ is a politician involved in local government.

3 hoard / horde

The miser kept a _____ of coins hidden under his bed.

4 wet / whet

They served him with an aperitif to_____ his appetite.

5 write / right / rite / wright

William Shakespeare was a play_____ .

III How many spelling mistakes can you find in the sentences below? Underline and correct each mistake.

1 Fortunately there were some lifeboys on the keyside. We grabbed one and through it into the water.

2 My grandmother taut me how to need doe and bake bred.

3 We had to laugh when Jerome started flexing his puny mussels on the beech.

4 Their doing there work over they're.

5 Practically the hole nation went into morning when Princess Diana dyed in a car accident.

(Answers: page 188)

26 Hyphens (-)

a A hyphen shows that we wish to treat two or more words as a single unit. A single unit formed of two or more words is known as a *compound* word.

   e.g. brother-in-law; X-ray; ice-skating; washing-up

b There are no fixed rules for using the hyphen with compound <u>nouns</u>. These may be written as one word (e.g. motorway), as two words (e.g. safety pin) or with a hyphen (e.g. lamp-post).

Quite often it is a question of personal choice (e.g. by-pass or bypass). An unfamiliar or confusing combination of words will, however, usually require a hyphen. We use a hyphen, for example, to distinguish between certain nouns and verbs (e.g. a take-away / to take away).

On the other hand, a familiar, straightforward combination of words will not usually require a hyphen.

   e.g. a shoe shop   a school teacher
       a department store   a farm worker

c We often use a hyphen with certain prefixes. A *prefix* is a word or a set of letters placed in front of a word.

                                                 (see Unit 33)

   e.g. <u>anti</u>-smoking; <u>mid</u>-air crash; <u>co</u>-operative; <u>non</u>-stop

d A compound <u>adjective</u> requires a hyphen.

   e.g. broken-hearted; big-headed

Any compound number (between 20 and 100) also requires a hyphen.

Note: With compound nouns, we can often choose whether to use a hyphen or not.

   e.g. a swimming pool; a swimming-pool; a dining room; a dining-room

---

> *Note:* If we use these words as an adjective, we have to use a hyphen.
>
> **e.g.** a swimming-pool attendant; a dining-room table

e Very often a group of words can <u>only</u> be used as a compound adjective when placed <u>before</u> a noun.

e.g. an out-of-work actor = the actor is out of work / a well-known actress = the actress is well known for her acting

TASK

I Complete the definitions below.

e.g. hair that reaches down to one's shoulders = shoulder-length hair

1 a boy with fair hair =

2 a girl who is twelve years old =

3 a flight that lasts eight hours =

4 a man who looks suspicious =

5 eyes that look sad =

II Add hyphens where necessary.

1 my great grandfather

2 a swimming pool

3 a break in

4 a waiting room

5 a hold up

6 forty four chairs

7 his ex wife

8 a non smoker

(Answers: page 189)

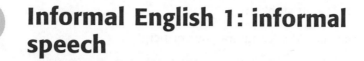

27 Informal English 1: informal speech

a Informal English (i.e. colloquial English) is the relaxed form of English that we use in speech and in personal letters. It is the sort of English that you may well find in advertisements and popular newspapers. In formal written English, however, you should be careful not to use language that is either too 'familiar' or too loose in meaning. Words like *loads*, *lots*, *stuff*, *crap* and *ain't* should be avoided. Equally, you should try to avoid – or, at least, to keep to a minimum – such overused words as *get* and *bit*.

b Whilst it is important to recognise that a clear distinction exists between spoken and written English, it is equally important not to make one's writing too stiff and formal. For instance, one cannot always avoid *get* in written English, and it is wrong to do so if the result is a stilted phrase or sentence.

Sometimes, too, a colloquial expression can add colour to one's writing. For example, the informal expression *he gave me the creeps* – although not as literary or 'elegant' as *he made my flesh creep* – conveys much more emotion than *he made me feel nervous*, and is slightly less theatrical than *he filled me with horror*.

TASK

Supply an alternative word or phrase for the words that have been underlined.

1 I <u>got</u> <u>loads of</u> presents from my cousin.

2 He <u>did</u> me out of £10.

3 It's <u>a good thing</u> we booked our tickets early.

4 I usually have a bath <u>last thing</u> before I go to bed.

5 <u>Say</u> you won the lottery, what would you do?

6 The test was <u>dead</u> easy.

7 She's <u>a bit</u> <u>stuck up</u>.

8 You should <u>stick</u> up for your principles.

9 She told him to <u>stick</u> to the point.

10 He asked us to wait for <u>a bit</u>.

(Answers: page 189)

28 Informal English 2: spoken and written English

a In spoken English, we tend to use *there's* with both singular and plural words or phrases.

   e.g. There's <u>someone</u> to see you.

       There's <u>some people</u> to see you.

In written English, we should only use *there's* (= there is) with a singular word or phrase.

   e.g. *There's* <u>a gentleman</u> waiting for you.

       There are <u>some gentlemen</u> waiting for you.

Be careful with *a lot of*:

   e.g. *There's* <u>a lot of noise</u> outside.

       There are <u>a lot of people</u> outside.

b The construction *should of...* does not exist in English grammar. After such verbs as *will, may, might, can, could, should, would* and *ought to*, we always use the infinitive form of a verb.

   e.g. He should <u>do</u> it. (present infinitive)

       He should <u>have done</u> it. (past infinitive)

When pronounced quickly, *should have done* sounds like *should of done* – and that is why it is such a common mistake to write *of* instead of *have* after these particular verbs.

c Avoid double negatives.

   e.g. I don't know nothing. (wrong)

       I know nothing. (correct)

       I don't know anything. (correct)

d The pronoun *me* is an object pronoun. The pronoun *I* is a subject pronoun.

   e.g. She invited Lorna and me.

       Lorna and I went together.

e In written English, you should never use *down* to mean 'to' or 'at'.

   e.g. Let's go down the pub. (informal English)

       They went to the pub. (written English)

f In written English, make sure you do not confuse adjectives with adverbs.

    e.g. It's a <u>real</u> pity he cannot come.

        (*real* is an adjective qualifying a noun)

        I am <u>really</u> sorry I cannot come.

        (*really* is an adverb qualifying an adjective)

        He is a <u>slow</u> driver. (*slow* is an adjective qualifying a noun)

        He drives <u>slowly</u>. (*slowly* is an adverb qualifying a verb)

                                                (see also Unit 5)

g In written English, always check subject-verb agreement.

    e.g. My brother <u>doesn't</u> eat meat.

        My father and my brother <u>don't</u> eat meat.

                                              (see also Unit 19)

h In written English, you should use *were* instead of *was* after *if*, *if only* and *I wish*.

    e.g. If I were you, I wouldn't buy that dress.

        If only he were here.

        I wish I were younger.

i In spoken English, we often use *like* with a subject and verb.

    e.g. "You look like you have seen a ghost."

        "He doesn't shout at us, like the other teachers do."

In written English, however, you should use *as* with a clause or prepositional phrase.

    e.g. As I have already indicated, we should…

        In this country, as in most countries, we…

If a clause follows a verb that carries the idea of 'give the impression that' or 'apparently', you should use *as if* or *as though*.

    e.g. She looked as if she had seen a ghost.

                                              (see also Unit 11)

j In written English, it is important not to confuse the <u>simple past</u> form of an irregular verb (e.g. did, broke, saw) with its <u>past participle</u> (e.g. done, broken, seen).

    e.g. I did the work yesterday.

        The work was done yesterday.

        I have done the work.

                                              (see also Unit 30)

Correct the sentences below.

1 There's plenty of things that you can do.

2 You should of told me earlier.

3 When he was questioned by the police, he said he hadn't seen nothing.

4 Me and Barry went swimming on Saturday.

5 We went down the park for a game of football.

6 I thought he would find the test very difficult, but he did it real quick and without a single mistake.

7 My mother and I was walking down the road when we heard a piercing shriek behind us.

8 If I was you, I'd see a doctor.

9 Like I've said before, I don't see why I should help her.

10 Trevor definitely took the money. I seen him do it.

(Answers: page 189)

29 Informal English 3: helpful hints

a Whether we use *who* or *whom* depends on word order. Following a preposition, *who* becomes *whom*.

    e.g. Who were you referring to? = To whom were you referring?
                                        (more formal English)

b Occasionally, you might need to convert an object pronoun (e.g. me, you, him) into a possessive pronoun (e.g. my, your, his) in front of a gerund (a *gerund* is a verbal noun ending in *-ing*). We do this to show that, rather than functioning in its own right, the pronoun is actually part of a noun phrase.

    e.g. I don't like <u>him</u>.
           I don't like <u>his interrupting me like that</u>.
           'I don't like *him*' means 'I don't like him as a person'.
           'I don't like *his interrupting me like that*' means 'I don't like *his interruptions*'.
           In this case, *interrupting* is not a verb but a verbal noun (or gerund): it looks like a verb, but is used like a noun.

c Do not give an adjective a double comparative form. Either an adjective will end in *-er* (e.g. bigger, smaller, brighter) or it will be preceded by *more* (e.g. more interesting, more intelligent).

d *fewer / less*

    ● Before a plural noun, you should use *fewer* rather than *less*.
      e.g. fewer jobs, fewer students, fewer people

    ● Use *fewer than* before a number of people or things.
      e.g. fewer than twenty students

    ● Use *less than* before an amount or measurement.
      e.g. less than twenty pounds a week / less than a hundred miles

e Note the following pattern:
    No sooner had I turned my back *than* they started making noise again.

f Always complete the first of two different verb forms – even if it means repeating the verb.

  e.g. I have never *spoken* and would never *speak* to her in such a way.

| TASK |

Below you will find some typical grammatical mistakes made in spoken English. Correct each mistake.

1 It's not the cost what worries me, it's the time it will take.

2 The thing what annoys me is the way she talks about me behind my back.

3 It's no use me telling him. He never listens to me.

4 He said he would show me a more quicker way of doing it.

5 Less than a hundred people attended the concert.

6 "My daughter's happiness is all what matters," he said.

7 I have never and would never do such a thing!

8 No sooner had I watered the plants in the garden then it began to rain.

(Answers: page 190)

Irregular verbs

a Usually we add *-ed* to a verb to put it into the past tense. There are, however, many exceptions. Many verbs are irregular and should be learnt by heart.

b Some one-syllable verbs do not have a separate past form. The verb remains the same in the past.

e.g. set – set

I normally <u>set</u> off for school at 8.30.

Yesterday, I <u>set</u> off at 8.15.

Here are some more examples of verbs that do not have a separate past form:

bet, bid, burst, cast, cost, cut, hit, hurt, let, put, read, shut, split, spread, upset

c The majority of irregular verbs can be broken down into particular groups with their own pattern(s). It is easier to remember the past form(s) of the more difficult irregular verbs if you can relate them to other verbs that have a similar pattern. For example, *to strive* (past forms: strove, striven) is like *to drive* (drove, driven). Similarly, *to stride* (past forms: strode, stridden) is like *to ride* (rode, ridden).

Some other common patterns are:

- cling – clung
  fling – flung
  sting – stung
  swing – swung
  wring – wrung

- bleed – bled
  breed – bred
  feed – fed
  flee – fled
  lead – led

- drink – drank – drunk
  ring – rang – rung
  sing – sang – sung
  spring – sprang – sprung
  stink – stank – stunk

- pay – paid
  lay – laid
  say – said (Note the pronunciation)

- bear – bore – born(e)
  swear – swore – sworn
  tear – tore – torn
  wear – wore – worn

- catch – caught
  teach – taught

- bring – brought
  buy – bought
  fight – fought
  seek – sought
  think – thought

- bind – bound
  find – found
  grind – ground
  wind – wound

- mow – mowed – mown
  sew – sewed – sewn
  show – showed – shown
  sow – sowed – sown

- draw – drew – drawn
  know – knew – known
  throw – threw – thrown

d All regular verbs have just one past form (e.g. play – played). Many irregular verbs also have just one past form (e.g. hear – heard). In other words, with most verbs the simple past form and the past participle are one and the same.

Some irregular verbs, however, have two separate past forms.
e.g. do – did (simple past) – done (past participle)

In order to avoid confusing these two forms in your writing, it is important to understand what the past participle is used for.

e The past participle has four basic functions:

- It is used with the verb *to have* to form the 'perfect' tenses.
  e.g. I *have done* it. (= present perfect)
  I *had seen* it. (= past perfect)

- It is used with the verb *to have* to form a past infinitive.
  e.g. I should *tell* her. (*tell* = present infinitive)
  I should *have told* her. (*have told* = past infinitive)

- It is used with the verb *to be* (and sometimes *to get*) when we wish to make a verb 'passive'.
  e.g. Samuel *was bitten* by the dog. = The dog bit Samuel.

- It can be used as an adjective.
  e.g. a *frozen* chicken
  a *broken* toy

f In standard English, it is wrong to use an irregular past participle as the main verb in a sentence. It is grammatically incorrect to write *he done it* or *she seen it*.

g Some irregular verbs cause particular spelling problems and/or do not fit readily into a convenient 'package' (see 'c'). These verbs should be learnt separately.

    e.g. bite (bit, bitten)   break (broke, broken)
           choose (chose, chosen)   forbid (forbade, forbidden)
           hide (hid, hidden)   shake (shook, shaken)
           slide (slid)   strike (struck)
           tread (trod, trodden)   write (wrote, written)

h Particular attention should be paid to *lay* and *lie* as they are very confusing.

- The verb *to lay* (past form: *laid*) is a transitive verb. This means that it is always followed by an object noun or pronoun.
  e.g. They have *laid* a new path in the front garden.
         He *laid* down the law.
         The hen *laid* three eggs yesterday.

- The verb *to lie* (past forms: *lay*, *lain*) is an intransitive verb. This means that it does not take an object. It is usually followed by a preposition / prepositional phrase.
  e.g. We were told the village *lay* in a picturesque valley.
         She *lay* down and tried to sleep.
         It had *lain* there for years.

- The verb *to lie* (past form: *lied*) means 'not to tell the truth'.
  e.g. I have never *lied* to you.

i When an irregular verb forms part of a compound verb, it changes in its usual way.
  eg. see (saw, seen): <u>foresee</u> (foresaw, foreseen)
    shine (shone): <u>outshine</u> (outshone)

TASK

I Look at the verbs that have been underlined. In which sentences are the verbs in the present tense? In which sentences are the verbs in the past tense?

1 I <u>bet</u> I know the answer.

2 He <u>bet</u> £100 on a horse called 'Fortune', and it finished last!

3 Although I eat a lot of chocolate, I never <u>put</u> on weight.

4 She <u>put</u> the dress on, looked in the mirror and realised that she had <u>put</u> on weight.

II Change the verbs in brackets into an appropriate past tense form.

1 The Romans had a law that (forbid) the wearing of trousers.

2 They (strive) valiantly to keep the enemy at bay.

3 She (lie) down on the sofa and tried to get a few minutes' sleep.

4 First, she (lay) some newspapers over the kitchen floor and then she (begin) to paint the walls.

5 That particular advertisement has (mislead) a lot of people.

6 Not wishing to be (sting) by the wasps, he (fling) the jam sandwiches into the river.

7 The branch (strike) me in the face and (break) my nose.

8 In his final years, he (seek) solace in drink.

9 He (stink) of beer, and we were all absolutely disgusted.

10 She (swim) to the life raft and (cling) desperately to its side, but then a huge wave (sweep) her away and she was never (see) again.

(Answers: page 190)

31 Loan words

a Over the years, the English language has 'borrowed' many foreign words and phrases. Many of these 'loan' words are very common ones and usually cause no problems of comprehension.

e.g. marmalade (Portuguese), ski (Norwegian), macho (Spanish), hamburger (German), algebra (Arabic)

Quite often, however, a common 'loan' word may be tricky to spell.

e.g. yacht (Dutch), yoghurt (Turkish), graffiti, paparazzi, ghetto, confetti, spaghetti (Italian), psychology, pneumonia, phenomenon, catastrophe (Greek)

b Some words which come from other languages have special plurals.

- Greek: crisis – crises; hypothesis – hypotheses; oasis – oases; criterion – criteria; phenomenon – phenomena

- Latin: cactus – cacti (*or* cactuses); formula – formulae (*or* formulas); fungus – fungi (*or* funguses); medium – media (*or* mediums in some contexts); nucleus – nuclei (*or* nucleuses); radius – radii (*or* radiuses); stimulus – stimuli; vertebra – vertebrae (*or* vertebras)

- French: bureau – bureaux (*or* bureaus); chateau – chateaux (*or* chateaus); gateau – gateaux (*or* gateaus)

> *Note:* From the point of view of style, it is preferable to use the original Latin and French plural forms rather than the anglicised forms given in brackets.

I Match each 'loan' word with its country of origin.

1	sauna	a	France
2	siesta	b	Spain
3	fjord	c	Greece
4	cuisine	d	Japan
5	kindergarten	e	Finland
6	cosmonaut	f	Germany
7	soprano	g	Norway
8	drama	h	Italy
9	karate	i	Russia

II Certain abbreviations in English are Latin in origin. Translate the following Latin phrases into English:

LATIN	Abbreviation		ENGLISH
Anno Domini	AD	=	
ante meridiem	a.m.	=	
exempli gratia	e.g.	=	
et cetera	etc.	=	
id est	i.e.	=	
nota bene	NB	=	
post meridiem	p.m.	=	
post scriptum	PS	=	
Requiescat in pace	RIP	=	

(Answers: page 190)

32 Loose English

a Look at the two sentences below. Each sentence begins with a participle clause.

Feeling tired and hungry, Rebecca asked if they could stop for a rest.
Founded in 1757, Ham School has a long and illustrious history.

The participle clause is formed with either a present participle (e.g. being, having) or a past participle (e.g. built, chosen) and is separated from the main clause by a comma. In the examples above, it is very clear that *Rebecca* is the subject of *feeling tired and hungry* and that *Ham School* is the subject of *founded in 1757*.

Now look at the following sentence:

Upset at the news, my mother tried to comfort me.

Who was upset? According to the sentence structure, it was *my mother*. Is that what the writer meant? In other words, the participle clause has been used too loosely and has created ambiguity.

When using a participle clause, make sure that the subject comes straight after the comma. Otherwise, you will end up with what is known as a 'dangling' participle.

The earlier sentence should have read:

Upset at the news, I turned to my mother for comfort.

b When using more than one verb, make sure that the tenses are in harmony.
   e.g. <u>Do</u> you mind if I <u>open</u> a window? | <u>Would</u> you mind if I <u>opened</u> a window?

c Since *the reason* already contains the idea of *because*, there is no need to repeat the idea in the second part of the sentence. Use the following patterns:

The main reason is that... | The reason (why) we are here today is that... | The reason for the delay is that the pilot has been taken ill.

d We normally use *do* to avoid repeating a verb.

   e.g. She works just as hard as he does.

   In British English, this does not apply in the case of *to have* or *to be*.

   e.g. She has her own point of view, just as he has.
         Xia Wang is Chinese and so is Lu Zuo.

e Be particularly careful with *what* and *than*. We do not use *what* after *than* except when *what* means 'that which / the things which'.

   e.g. My younger brother can swim faster than I can.
         This is better than what we ate yesterday.

f Note the following patterns:

   The fish he caught this morning was *twice the size* of the one he caught last week.

   The fish he caught this morning was *twice as big as* the one he caught last week.

   Logically, we should follow the same pattern for *three times, four times,* etc.

   e.g. The fish he caught this morning was *three times as big* as the one he caught last week.

g When describing where someone is seated, it is incorrect to say that someone *is sat* there.

In Standard English, we should use the present participle (sitting) with *to be*.
e.g. I <u>was sitting</u> at my desk, doing my homework.

TASK

I Correct the following sentences:

1 "Would you mind if I use your bathroom?" she asked.

2 The reason why he is so tired is because he has not had a proper break for years.

3 She has a more interesting job than he does.

4 She can type faster than what I can.

5 France is three times larger than England.

6 She was sat by the window, reading a magazine.

II In only one of the sentences below has a participle clause been used correctly. Tick that sentence. How can the other sentences be improved?

1 Being sensible, I am sure that Katie will not do anything foolish.

2 Being such a miserable morning, we decided not to go to the beach.

3 Having been kept awake most of the night by the noise next door, Jessica was in a foul mood that morning.

4 Having suggested the idea in the first place, Mr Fowler could not understand why Ms Hodgkins had then objected to the plan.

(Answers: page 190)

33 Negative prefixes

a   Some words seem very difficult to spell at first sight, but are actually fairly straightforward once you realise that they consist of a negative prefix and a whole word.
    e.g. *dis-* + satisfied = dissatisfied; *dis-* + appointed = disappointed

b   Look carefully at the list of negative prefixes below and the examples alongside.

  • *im-* + moral = immoral; *im-* + possible = impossible;
    im- + polite = impolite
  • *in-* + numerable = innumerable; *in-* + accurate = inaccurate
  • *ir-* + resistible = irresistible; *ir-* + rational = irrational
  • *il-* + literate = illiterate; *il-* + logical = illogical
  • *un-* + natural = unnatural; *un-* + occupied = unoccupied
  • *dis-* + appear = disappear; *dis-* + organised = disorganised
  • *mis-* + spell = misspell; *mis-* + place = misplace

c   The general meaning of a negative prefix is 'not' or 'opposite of'. Be careful, however, with certain words that can take different negative prefixes with different shades of meaning.
    e.g. misused   = used wrongly, badly (e.g. the *misuse* of power)
        disused   = no longer being used (e.g. a *disused* mine)
        unused   = not having been used (e.g. an *unused* stamp)
        unused to   = unaccustomed to (e.g. He is *unused to* heavy exercise.)

        disinterested = neutral, impartial (e.g. a *disinterested* observer)
        uninterested = not interested (e.g. *Uninterested* in studying, she failed the examination.)

I Complete the sentences below by using the words given in italics.

misused | disused | unused

1 The old, _____ church was converted into a family home.

2 Here's a(n) _____ envelope. Will it do?

3 They claimed that he had _____ his authority.

uninterested | disinterested

4 During the dispute he claimed to be a(n) _____ observer.

5 I thought he might like to play some games on the computer, but he looked totally _____ when I suggested the idea.

II Add a suitable negative prefix to each word.

1 _____ patient		6 _____ mortal
2 _____ considerate		7 _____ replaceable
3 _____ lead		8 _____ efficient
4 _____ respectful		9 _____ approve
5 _____ relevant		10 _____ behave

(Answers: page 191)

34 Nouns 1: noun endings

a The suffixes *-er*, *-or* and *-ar* are often misspelt because they usually sound the same. As you read the rules of thumb below, bear in mind that the commonest suffix of the three is *-er*.

b Nouns that end in *-er* and *-or* are known as 'agent' nouns because, generally speaking, they show the specific job, occupation or function of a person or thing.

  e.g. a *singer* is someone who sings (for a living); a *translator* is someone who translates; a *duplicator* is a machine that duplicates things

c An 'agent' noun may also show the specific activity that someone is involved in.

  e.g. a *smuggler* is someone who is involved in smuggling goods; a *visitor* is someone who is paying a visit; a *competitor* is someone involved in a competition

d A technical word of Latin origin is more likely to end in *-or*.

  e.g. calculator, incubator, duplicator, processor, monitor, transistor, projector

---

Note, however, the following: printer, computer, photocopier, stapler, typewriter, container.

---

e When referring to a person's trade or occupation, *-er* is more common than *-or*.

  e.g. *-er*: boxer, carpenter, fighter, hunter, interpreter, painter, teacher, writer

  -or: decorator, sailor, tailor

f On the other hand, formal positions or people's titles are often – but not always – denoted by *-or*.

  e.g. ambassador, author, chancellor, conqueror, councillor, counsellor, emperor, professor, proprietor, rector, senator, solicitor, sponsor, successor, suitor, surveyor

g Occasionally an agent word may be spelt with either -*er* or -*or*. In such cases, -*er* denotes a person.

    e.g. a *resister* is someone who resists; a *resistor* is an electrical device

> *Note:* Do not confuse a *miner* (one who works in a mine) with a *minor* (a young person not yet legally an adult).

h -*ar* is found at the end of just a few agent nouns. The main ones are *beggar*, *burglar*, *liar* and *scholar*.

i Other common nouns ending in -*ar* include: altar, calendar, caterpillar, cellar, vinegar, collar, dollar, grammar, guitar, hangar, mortar, nectar, pillar, sugar, vicar

> *Note:* Be careful not to confuse the following words:
> **e.g.** an *altar* (noun) is found in a church / to *alter* (verb) means to change; a *hangar* (noun) is where one keeps aircraft / a *hanger* (noun) is used for hanging up clothes

j The suffixes -*ence* and -*ance* are used to form abstract nouns. There is no easy way of distinguishing between these two suffixes, but there are certain guidelines that are worth bearing in mind:

- -*ence* follows a soft *c* or *g*.
  e.g. innocence, adolescence, intelligence

- -*ance* follows a hard *c* or *g*.
  e.g. significance, elegance, arrogance

  Exceptions: allegiance, vengeance

- A noun will usually end in -*ence* rather than -*ance* if the root verb connected with it ends in -*ere*.
  e.g. interfere – interference; cohere – coherence; revere – reverence

  Exception: persevere – perseverance

- A noun will usually end in -*ance* rather than -*ence* if the verb connected with it ends in -*ear*, -*ure* or -*y*.
  e.g. appear – appearance; assure – assurance; insure – insurance; rely – reliance; ally – alliance; defy – defiance

Note: If a root verb ends in a consonant +-*y*, the *y* will change to *i* before -*ance*.

k Many words follow a logical pattern from adjective to noun.
e.g. independ<u>ent</u> – independ<u>ence</u>; confid<u>ent</u> – confid<u>ence</u>; relev<u>ant</u> – relev<u>ance</u>; attend<u>ant</u> – attend<u>ance</u>

(See also Unit 49)

l Note carefully the spelling of each of the following verbs and nouns:
e.g. maintain – maintenance; remember – remembrance; hinder – hindrance; excel – excellence; admit – admittance

TASK

I Where a word is incomplete, add one of the following suffixes: -*er*, -*or*, -*ar*.

1 William the Conquer _____ invaded England in 1066.

2 The direct _____ of a play or film has the same task as the conduct _____ of an orchestra. He or she rehearses the act _____ s and helps them to interpret their parts.

3 The transist _____ radio was invented in 1948.

4 When Gustave Eiffel designed his famous Eiffel Tower in Paris, object _____ s said it would be a danger to birds.

5 The first steam engine was built in 1805 by the English invent _____ Richard Trevithick.

6 James Cook (1728–79) was an English explor _____ and navigat _____ .

7 By about 2800 BC the Egyptians had invented a calend _____ to keep track of time.

8 The Roman Emper _____ Nero was the only competit _____ to be awarded first place in an Olympic competition without winning or even finishing the race.

II Complete each sentence by forming an appropriate noun from the verb given in brackets.

1 His sudden ＿＿＿＿＿＿ mystified the whole village. (disappear)

2 He proved to be more of a ＿＿＿＿＿＿ than a help. (hinder)

3 The house was very old and needed a lot of ＿＿＿＿＿＿ . (maintain)

4 The school he attends is noted for its academic ＿＿＿＿＿＿ . (excel)

5 The notice said, 'Private – no ＿＿＿＿＿＿ '. (admit)

(Answers: page 191)

35 Nouns 2: formation and spelling

a When forming nouns with *-ment*, it is important to remember that we usually keep *-e* before *-ment*.
   e.g. excite – exciting – exci<u>te</u>ment

    Exception: argue – arg<u>um</u>ent

b When forming nouns with *-ness*, remember that *-y* will usually change to *-i*.
   e.g. nasty – nastiness; tidy – tidiness; happy – happiness

    Exceptions: dryness, shyness

c When we add *-ness* to a word ending in *-n*, we end up with *nn* in the middle of the word.
   e.g. openness, meanness, drunkenness

Note: A female lion = a lioness (= lion + ess)

---

d Certain nouns ending in *-tion* are tricky to spell for a variety of reasons. It is best to learn the following words by heart:
   - deceive – deception; describe – description; receive – reception

   - add – addition; compete – competition; define – definition; oppose – opposition; recognise – recognition; repeat – repetition

   - abbreviate – abbreviation; accommodate – accommodation; accuse – accusation; assassinate – assassination; associate – association; cancel – cancellation; despair – desperation; exaggerate – exaggeration; explain – explanation; imagine – imagination; pronounce – pronunciation; separate – separation

e Note carefully the following spelling patterns (adjective – noun):
   - gener*ous* – gener*osity*; curi*ous* – curi*osity*
   - responsib*le* – responsib*ility*; ab*le* – ab*ility*
   - hum*orous* – hum*our*; vig*orous* – vig*our*; glam*orous* – glam*our*
   - an*xious* – an*xiety*; va*rious* – va*riety*
   - lo*ng* – le*ngth*; stro*ng* – str*ength*

f Most nouns ending in *-ssion* are formed from verbs with the following endings:
- *-mit*: admit – admission; permit – permission; transmit – transmission
- *-cede* or *-ceed*: recede – recession; proceed – procession

g Most nouns ending in *-sion* are formed from verbs with the following endings:
- *-de*: collide – collision; persuade – persuasion; provide – provision
- *-ere*: adhere – adhesion; cohere – cohesion
- *-nd*: expand – expansion; extend – extension; pretend – pretension

  Exceptions: attend – attention; contend – contention; intend – intention

- *-pel*: compel – compulsion; expel – expulsion; repel – repulsion
- *-use*: confuse – confusion; fuse – fusion
- *-vert*: convert – conversion; divert – diversion; pervert – peversion
- *-vise*: supervise – supervision; revise – revision

TASK

I To complete each sentence below, form a noun ending in *-tion* from the word in brackets:

1 Are you going to enter the swimming _____? (compete)

2 He needs to improve his _____ . (pronounce)

3 The place has changed beyond _____ . (recognise)

4 His proposal met with a lot of _____ . (oppose)

5 She gave the police a detailed _____ of the man. (describe)

6 She demanded an _____ . (explain)

II Complete each sentence by forming an appropriate noun from the adjective in brackets:

1 Her strange appearance aroused our _____ . (curious)

2 He has no sense of _____ . (responsible)

3 I like his sense of _____ . (humorous)

4 They have caused us a great deal of _____ . (anxious)

5 Does he have the _____ and stamina to run a marathon? (strong)

III Complete each sentence by forming an appropriate noun (ending in *-sion* or *-ssion*) from the verb in brackets.

1 Do you have _____ to be here? (permit)

2 The vehicles were involved in a head-on _____ . (collide)

3 He was caught in _____ of illegal drugs. (possess)

4 What was the cause of the _____ ? (explode)

5 Are you going to do any _____ for the exams? (revise)

(Answers: page 191)

36 Passive voice

a Look carefully at the passage below. The verb groups in italics are examples of the passive voice.

The tomato – fruit or vegetable?

Strangely enough, the tomato *is classed* as a fruit by botanists because it contains seeds. It *is regarded* as a berry, like the raspberry or strawberry. When tomatoes *were first introduced* into Europe from Peru, they *were called* 'love apples'.

b The English language has two basic 'voices': the <u>active</u> and the <u>passive</u>.

When we refer to the active voice, we simply mean that the words in a sentence follow the usual pattern of *subject* = (the agent responsible for the action of the verb) + *verb* + *object* (= the person or thing affected by the action).

e.g. In 1885 Gottlieb Daimler built the first petrol-driven motorcycle.

The passive, on the other hand, puts emphasis on the person or thing affected by the verb rather than on the agent. If we change a sentence from active to passive, the object in the active sentence will become the subject in the passive sentence.

e.g. The first petrol-driven motorcycle was built by Gottlieb Daimler in 1885.

1 Not all active sentences with objects can be passivised.

e.g. ✓ She lacks confidence.

✗ Confidence is lacked by her.

✓ The baby resembles the father.

✗ The father is resembled by the baby.

✓ This dress does not fit you.

✗ You are not fitted by this dress.

| ✓ | He has a pretty wife. |

| ✗ | A pretty wife is had by him. |

2 Sentences with reflective, reciprocal or possessive pronouns as objects cannot be passivized.

e.g. | ✓ | The Queen could see herself in the mirror. |

| ✗ | Herself could be seen in the mirror. |

| ✓ | They held each other tightly. |

| ✗ | Each other were held tightly. |

| ✓ | The bald doctor shook his head. |

| ✗ | His head was shaken by the bald doctor. |

c The passive is formed with the appropriate tense of the verb 'to be' + past participle (e.g. known, hidden, bitten).
e.g. The roof is being repaired. / The roof hasn't been repaired yet.

In informal English, it is possible to use 'get' + past participle.
e.g. One of my mates got arrested last night.

You should, however, avoid using 'get' + past participle when writing formal or academic English.

d As well as emphasising the real subject in a sentence, the passive is used as follows:
  • When there is no need to mention the agent (because, for example, it is obvious, unknown or unimportant)
    e.g. Anthony *was taken* to hospital last night.
          Basketball *was played* for the first time in December 1891, in America.

  • In describing processes or scientific experiments (where the action or event is more important than the agent)
    e.g. Petrol *is made* from oil in a refinery. The oil *is heated* to produce petrol vapour, and the petrol vapour condenses to give petrol.

- In formal written English (in order to avoid such indefinite pronouns as 'you' or 'they')

  e.g. You can't sell alcohol without a licence. (informal)
  Alcohol *cannot be sold* without a licence. (formal)
  They grow rice in China. (informal)
  Rice *is grown* in China. (formal)

- To make a statement sound more formal, impersonal or official

  e.g. Customers *are reminded* that goods will *not be exchanged* without a valid receipt.

- In academic and formal English, to emphasise objectivity and to avoid such loose phrases as 'some people say' or 'a lot of people think'

> *Note:* To stress objectivity, the neutral pronoun 'it' is often used to make a statement sound more formal and less personal.
> **e.g.** It is *often argued* that... / It *has been suggested* that...
> She *is thought* to be the finest actress in the world.

TASK

Change the verbs in brackets into the passive. In each case, be careful to choose the correct tense.

1 Many stars in the universe are bigger than our sun. They (know) as 'blue giants'. The biggest star (estimate) to be over 700 times as big as the sun.

2 Cricket (believe) to have originated in England in the fifteenth century, and from old newspapers we are able to see that cricket matches (advertise) in the early 1700s. The first recorded county cricket match (play) in 1719.

3 The Sahara was not always a desert. Millions of years ago it (cover) in grasslands and forests.

4 Only about a tenth of the Sahara Desert (cover) with wind-blown sand. The rest is gravel plains, plateaux and mountains.

5   The Greek doctor Hippocrates (know) as the 'Father of Medicine'.
    He insisted upon scientific observation and detailed record-making
    of each illness he came across. His findings still (read) and (refer) to
    by today's medical profession.

6   The first hovercraft, SR-N1, (launch) in 1959. It (design) by an
    Englishman, Christopher Cockerell, who (knight) ten years later for
    his invention.

(Answers: page 191)

37 Plain English

a Nothing is gained by using unnecessarily complicated language. It will sound pompous and will usually be incomprehensible. Recently, a supermarket chain advertised for 'ambient replenishment assistants'. One could be forgiven for thinking that such a grandiose title denoted a highly-skilled job. In fact, they were looking for people to stack shelves.

In the United States, the inability to speak a foreign language is officially labelled 'a negative dialogue capability situation'.

Such gobbledegook should be avoided at all times in your own writing.

b Try not to use 'big' words in order to impress the reader. The result often sounds pretentious.

   e.g. We are endeavouring to ascertain her whereabouts. = We are trying to find out where she is.

c A 'euphemism' is a word or phrase that is gentler or less direct than the one normally used to refer to something unpleasant or embarrassing.

   e.g. He has passed on / away. = He is dead.

Euphemisms have always been part of the English language. However, the modern trend of obsessively rephrasing anything that is remotely offensive or unpleasant has given rise to such expressions as 'a follicly challenged person' (= someone who is bald) and 'to subject a department to over-ratio amelioration' (= to reduce the number of staff in a department). The use of such ugly terminology is not recommended.

d When writing English, you should follow the advice given by Sir Ernest Gowers, the author of a very useful book, *The Complete Plain Words*: 'Be short, be simple, be human.'

I Below you will find six genuine examples of 'officially correct' language used by modern bureaucrats. In each case, what is being described? To help you decide, select your answers from the list given underneath (*a* – *i*). There are three extra words in the list.

1 'A wheeled vehicle designed for the transport in a seated or semi-recumbent position of one or two babies who are placed inside a body of boat or box-like shape.'

2 'Festive embellishments of an illuminary nature.'

3 'A horticultural festive element.'

4 'A grain-consuming unit.'

5 'A domestic service engineer.'

6 'An appliance for milling wooden dowels up to 10 millimetres in length.'

a	a Christmas tree	**f**	a sheep, cow or pig
b	Christmas lights	**g**	a housewife
c	a car	**h**	a plumber
d	a pram	**i**	a pencil sharpener
e	a tractor		

II Below you will find some genuine examples of language used by modern business executives. What do all these statements mean in plain English?

1 "We are giving you a stimulated secondary opportunity to develop your career."

2 "We have decided to dehire you."

3 "You have been deselected."

4 "We are offering you accelerated retirement."

5 "We are downsizing your department."

(Answers: page 192)

38 Plurals

a To make most nouns plural, simply add *-s*.
   e.g. place – places; ski – skis; pen – pens; girl – girls

b Add *-es* to words ending in *-ch, -sh, -s, -ss, -x*. These are known as sibilant (= hissing) consonants, and an *-e* is required to ease pronunciation.
   e.g. bench – benches; dish – dishes; gas – gases; dress – dresses; fox – foxes; brush – brushes; church – churches; box – boxes

 Exceptions: 1 loch – lochs; stomach – stomachs
2 oasis – oases; crisis – crises
3 cactus – cacti *or* cactuses; radius – radii *or* radiuses; fungus – fungi *or* funguses (both plural forms are acceptable)

c For most words that end in *-o*, simply add *-s* for the plural form. These include:

- words of Spanish or Italian origin, especially those connected with music
   e.g. cello – cellos; piano – pianos; soprano – sopranos; concerto – concertos

- words where there is another vowel in front of the *-o*
   e.g. studio – studios; patio – patios; zoo – zoos; cuckoo – cuckoos; kangaroo – kangaroos; radio – radios

- words that are abbreviations
   e.g. rhino – rhinos (rhino = rhinoceros); hippo – hippos (hippo = hippopotamus); kilo – kilos (kilo = kilogram); photo – photos (photo = photograph)

There are some exceptions:

- Certain words ending in *-o* take *-es* for the plural form.
   e.g. domino – dominoes; echo – echoes; hero – heroes; potato – potatoes; tomato – tomatoes

- Certain words ending in -*o* take either -*s* or -*es*.

  e.g. mango – mangoes *or* mangos; tornado – tornadoes
  or tornados; volcano – volcanoes *or* volcanos

d For words ending in a consonant +-*y*, change the -*y* to -*i* and add -*es*.

  e.g. baby – babies; lorry – lorries; story – stories;
  cherry – cherries; city – cities; party – parties

e For words ending in a vowel +-*y*, simply add -*s*.

  e.g. journey – journeys; monkey – monkeys; ray – rays;
  chimney – chimneys

f For words ending in -*f* or -*fe*, change the -*f* or -*fe* to -*ves*.

  e.g. loaf – loaves; leaf – leaves; thief – thieves; life – lives;
  shelf – shelves; knife – knives

 Exceptions: chiefs, handkerchiefs, roofs, cliffs.

  - A few words may end in either -*fs* or -*ves*.

    e.g. dwarf – dwarfs *or* dwarves; scarf – scarfs *or* scarves;
    hoof – hoofs *or* hooves

g Particular attention should be paid to the following words of
foreign origin:

  e.g. phenomenon – phenomena; stratum – strata; medium – media;
  chateau – chateaux*; bureau – bureaux*; gateau – gateaux*

  (* It is also possible to use -*s* instead of -*x* for these words.)

h Be careful with certain words that have hyphens.

  e.g. passer-by – passers-by; son-in-law – sons-in-law; lay-by – lay-
  bys

i Some words do not change at all. They are both singular and plural.

  e.g. species, series, sheep, deer, salmon, fish

j Some plural words need to be learnt separately.

  e.g. man – men; foot – feet; goose – geese; tooth – teeth;
  louse – lice; mouse – mice; ox – oxen

k Do not use an apostrophe +*s* (*'s*) to make a noun plural.

  ☒ She bought some apple's, pear's and orange's.

  ☑ She bought some apples, pears and oranges.

TASK

I Give the plural form of the underlined words.

1 <u>Zoo</u> are places where wild animals are kept and exhibited.

2 <u>Kangaroo</u> are found in Australia.

3 Contrary to what people believe, elephants are not afraid of <u>mouse</u>.

4 <u>Tomato</u> were first introduced into Europe from Peru.

5 Lord Nelson is regarded as one of Britain's greatest <u>hero</u>.

6 <u>Rhino</u> have been known to live for over 40 years.

7 Malaria is transmitted by <u>mosquito</u>.

8 All the islands of Hawaii are actually the tops of great <u>volcano</u>.

II Match each phrase in column A with a suitable noun from column B, made plural.

A	B
a herd of	goose
a gang of	sheep
a gaggle of	ox
a flock of	workman
a set of	false tooth

(Answers: page 192)

Prepositions

a Prepositions are words such as *in, of, to, at, from, between* and *with*.

b After a preposition, the correct pronoun to use is an object pronoun (i.e. me, you, him, her, it, us, them). In the same way that we say *between him and her* (not *between he and she*), so we say *between you and me* (not *between you and I*).

c *of / off*
When distinguishing between the prepositions *of* and *off*, we should remember the following basic points:

- The two words are pronounced differently; *of* ends in a hard sound (= v), whereas *off* has a gentle *f* sound.

- The commonest way of showing a relationship between words is to use *of*.
  e.g. a cup *of* tea; the end *of* the road; the first day *of* the month

- The basic meaning of *off* is 'away from'. It is also the opposite of *on*.
  e.g. Keep *off* the grass. = Do not walk on the grass.

- We associate *off* with movement.
  e.g. They set off early.

d *in / into*; *out / out of*
- We use *into* (= one word) when we want to show where someone or something has gone.
  e.g. He slipped and fell *in*.
  He slipped and fell *into* the pond.

- We use *out of* when we want to show from where someone or something has come.
  e.g. He got *out*.
  He got *out of* the taxi.

e   When talking about the main feature / element of something, we use *in* after *consist*.
e.g. His work *consists in* helping refugees.

f   'The bottle is *made of* glass' means that glass has been used to make the bottle (and we can still see the glass).

'Glass is *made from* sand' means that sand is used to make glass (and, once this happens, the sand can never be sand again).

g   We use *on* with *improvement* when we are making a comparison.
e.g. Model B is a distinct *improvement on* Model A. (i.e. Model B is much better than Model A.)

h   When *surprised* is clearly being used as an adjective, use *at* rather than *by*.
e.g. I am surprised at him. (i.e. I find his attitude / behaviour surprising.)

When *surprised* can be seen either as an adjective or as part of a passive construction, use either *at* or *by*.
e.g. He was surprised by / at her attitude.
    (similarly: amazed at, astonished at)

i   We compare A *with* B to show their differences. A poet, however, will compare A *to* B as a simile or illustration. As a joining phrase, *compared* can be followed either by *with* or *to*.
e.g. Your house is luxurious compared with / to ours.

j   Note the following patterns:
   • He *replaced* the faulty light-bulb *with* a new one.
     He *substituted* a new light-bulb *for* the faulty one.

   • to differ *from*
     to be different *from* / *to* (not *than*)

   • The committee *consists of* six members.
     The committee *is composed of* six members.
     The committee *comprises* six members.
     (no preposition after *comprise*)

k • <u>in the end</u> = eventually
  <u>at the end</u> = (of a road / film / book) indicates 'where'

• to agree <u>with</u> something = to approve of something (e.g. an idea)
  to agree <u>to</u> something = to say 'yes' to / to assent to something
  (e.g. a proposal)

• <u>on</u> principle = as a matter of principle
  <u>in</u> principle = in theory

l • you rob / cure / deprive somebody <u>of</u> something

• to go in search <u>of</u> something = to search <u>for</u> something

• to be fed up *with* ... = to be tired *of* ...

■ TASK

I Correct any mistakes in the sentences below.

1 Please keep this to yourself. This is strictly between you and I.

2 The new committee will comprise of ten members: seven
   students and three teachers.

3 For me, the beauty of this poem consists of its unusual imagery.

4 Glass is made of sand.

5 The criminal's plan was to substitute fake diamonds with the
   ones he intended to steal.

6 You have got away with it so far, but they will catch you at the
   end.

II Underline the correct alternative in brackets.

1 He's just bought a new set (of / off) tools.

2 We set (of / off) at six o'clock the following morning.

3 A bottle is usually made (of / off) glass.

4 She threw him (out / out of) the house.

5 He walked (in / into) the room and sat down.

6 He got (in / into) the car and drove off.

7 He fell (of / off) his bicycle.

8 He jumped (out / out of) bed.

9 The bird flew (out / out of) the window and disappeared.

10 She went (in / into) the kitchen and made a sandwich.

(Answers: page 192)

40 **Regular verbs in the past**

a We use the suffix *-ed* to indicate the past form of a regular verb.

b If a one-syllable verb ends in a single vowel and consonant, we double the final consonant when we add *-ed*.
   e.g. stop – stopped; fit – fitted; pat – patted; tap – tapped; hop – hopped; hug – hugged

 Exceptions: We never double the letters *-w, -x, -y*.
   e.g. bow – bowed; fix – fixed; play – played

c If a one-syllable verb already ends in *-e*, we just add *-d*.
   e.g. hope – hoped; stare – stared

d If a one-syllable verb ends in two vowels and a consonant, we do not double the final consonant.
   e.g. steer – steered; peer – peered; fear – feared; pour – poured

e If a verb has more than one syllable and ends in a single vowel and consonant, we usually double the final consonant <u>if the last syllable is stressed</u>.
   e.g. admit – admitted; prefer – preferred; occur – occurred; *but* offer – offered; open – opened; happen – happened; benefit – benefited; visit – visited; tamper – tampered (The stress does not fall on the last syllable)

> *Note:* When considering words like *equip*, the letters *qu* count as a single consonant.
> **e.g.** equip – equipped

Exceptions: **1** handicap – handicapped; kidnap – kidnapped; worship – worshipped; program – programmed

   2 Even though the last syllable is not stressed, we always double the *-l* when adding *-ed* to words ending in one vowel and *-l*.
   e.g. travel – travelled; control – controlled

f If a verb ends in a consonant *+-y*, we change the y to *i* when we add *-ed*.

e.g.   try – tried; cry – cried; carry – carried; hurry – hurried

g If a verb ends in *-ic*, we add *k* before *-ed*.

e.g.   picnic – picnicked; panic – panicked

(See also Unit 45)

▐ TASK ▐

Each verb in brackets should end in *-ed*. As you change each verb, make any other necessary changes (e.g. doubling the last letter; changing *y* to *i*).

> As Lieutenant Kowolski (sip) his coffee, he carefully (study) the man who was sitting opposite him. It was at times like these, he (admit) to himself, that he (envy) those officers who had (incur) the wrath of Captain Reilley and been (transfer) to traffic-control duties.
>
> "Let's get this straight," (drawl) the lieutenant. "You say that this has (occur) more than once."
>
> "Yes, sir," (reply) the man. "It has (happen) three times now."
>
> "And each time, you say, you were (carry) off against your will."
>
> "That is correct, officer. I (beg) them to let me go, but they (force) me to go with them. Naturally, I (offer) no resistance. That's why I wasn't (harm) physically."
>
> "Why didn't you report the first incident?"
>
> "They (order) me not to."
>
> "I see. So, you have been (kidnap) three times."
>
> "That's right, officer."
>
> "By aliens, you say."
>
> "Yes, sir. Creatures from outer space."
>
> "And each time, you (travel) to Mars and back in a cigar-shaped vessel. Is that correct?"
>
> "That's correct, officer."
>
> "Good heavens!" (mutter) Lieutenant Kowolski.

(Answers: page 192)

41 Relative pronouns: *who, which, whose, whom*

a *who / which*

We can use *who* or *which* as 'joining words' (like links in a chain!). The important point to remember is that *who* comes immediately after a 'person' noun or pronoun, and *which* comes immediately after any other type of noun.

e.g. I think it was <u>Michael who</u> phoned.

(Michael = a 'person' noun)

A saltwater fish is <u>a fish which</u> can only live in the sea.

(a 'fish' is not a person)

b *who / whose*

Whose is a 'possessive' word. We can use *whose* as a 'joining' word when we want to show a *possessive* relationship between a 'person' noun and a noun that immediately follows.

e.g. At the concert last night, I spoke to <u>a boy whose brother</u> plays in a group.

c *who / whom*

Whom is a very formal word. In the old days, there were many complicated rules for when you should or shouldn't use *whom*. Nowadays, we are more relaxed about the word. All you need to remember is that *who* becomes *whom* when you have a preposition in front of *who*. (see Unit 39)

e.g. <u>Who</u> is she going out with? (= normal, informal English)

<u>With whom</u> is she going out? (= very formal English)

Complete the gaps below with *who, which, whose* or *whom*:

1 The African ostrich, _____ is the largest of all living birds, cannot fly at all.

2 Some crocodiles will not only attack anyone _____ comes near them in the water, but they will run up on the land in pursuit of their victims, grab them and carry them back into the water!

3 The jellyfish is an animal _____ doesn't have a skeleton. It doesn't have a brain either!

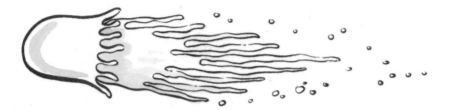

4 That's the girl _____ took my bicycle.

5 That's the girl _____ bicycle was stolen.

6 Ann: I've just received some money.

   Sue: _____ from?

7 Dave: I've just received some money.

   Mark: From _____ ?

8 People say that John Montagu, the 4th Earl of Sandwich (1718–92), was the man _____ invented sandwiches.

(Answers: page 192)

42   Semicolons (;)

a The semicolon is stronger than a comma but weaker than a full stop. Sometimes two separate clauses are so closely related that we do not want to write them as separate sentences. In such cases, we can use the semicolon. Very often, there is a linking word or phrase before the second clause.

    e.g. I am sure he took it; in fact, I am positive he did.

         Nobody really expected us to win; nevertheless, it was disappointing to lose.

b The semicolon can be used between two neatly balanced or contrasting statements.

    e.g. 'Forty is the old age of youth; fifty is the youth of old age.'
(Victor Hugo)

         Arctic foxes are white; European foxes are red.

         The Aborigines are native to Australia; the Maoris are native to New Zealand.

c We use a semicolon instead of a comma to group parts of a sentence that contains many commas.

    e.g. For his daughter, he bought a dress; for his son, a watch; and for his wife, a silver bracelet.

TASK

In each sentence below, place a semicolon (;) where appropriate.

1 'Advice is seldom welcome and those who want it the most always like it the least.'
(Lord Chesterfield)

2 Chess is one of the oldest games in the world so old in fact that no one knows who invented it.

(Answers: page 193)

43 **Spoken and written English**

There are certain grammatical mistakes which are very common in informal speech. Be aware of these mistakes and try to avoid making them in your own writing.

a Whether we use *who* or *whom* depends on word order. Following a preposition, *who* becomes *whom*.

    e.g. Who were you referring to? = To whom were you referring? (more formal English)

b Double negatives

    Be really careful when using 'negative' words (such as *no, no one, nobody* and *nothing*). Since these are negative, they do not require a negative verb.

    e.g. I saw nobody. / I saw no one. / He did nothing. / There is no milk left.

    If we decide to make the verb negative, then *no* + word becomes *any* + word.

    e.g. I didn't see anybody. / I didn't see anyone. / He didn't do anything. / There isn't any milk left.

c *My brother and I / me and my brother*

    Before a verb, use *I*. After a verb or preposition, use *me*.

    e.g. My brother and I built a snowman in the back garden. She brought some presents for me and my brother.

d *don't / doesn't, was / were*

    Make absolutely sure that you use the correct part of a verb.

    e.g. I don't; you don't; we / they don't; he / she / it <u>doesn't</u>; I was; he / she / it was; we <u>were</u>; you <u>were</u>; they <u>were</u>

e Unlike many other languages, the English language is not always written in the same way as it is pronounced or spoken.

In informal speech, people often say things like *gonna*, *wanna*, *gotta*, *dunno*.

In standard written English, these words should be written as *going to*, *want to*, *got to* and *don't know*.

f Normally, *all* becomes *al* when added to another word.
e.g. almost, altogether, always, already

However, you should always spell *all right* as two separate words. The spelling *alright* is not acceptable in standard written English.

(See also Unit 52)

g In informal speech, the letters *th* are often mispronounced and may sound like *f* or *v*.
e.g. "my muvver"; "he's a fief"; "I fink"

In standard written English, spelling must be correct.
e.g. my mother; he's a thief; I think

This is particularly important with words that may change their meaning if you misspell them.
e.g. fought / thought; deaf / death; fink / think; free / three

h Vowel sounds are tricky in English. Spelling mistakes are often made when we simply write down the words as they sound.

e.g. ✗ villige, cottige, cabbige, grammer, calender

✓ village, cottage, cabbage, grammar, calendar

✗ responsable, definate, seperate, oppisite

✓ responsible, definite, separate, opposite

Some words are spelt differently in American English.
e.g. center (centre); theater (theatre); color (colour); favorite (favourite); neighbor (neighbour)

Be aware of this problem, and when in doubt use a dictionary.

I Below are some examples of informal speech. In each case there is a grammatical mistake. Can you correct them?

1 He is someone in who I have complete faith.

2 I didn't see nobody.

3 There's no point in asking her. She don't know.

4 Me and Susan, Ayesha, Sarah and Kiran went to a disco on Saturday night.

5 Me and my brother go swimming every Saturday.

II Rewrite the sentences below in standard written English.

e.g. "Get outta here!" = "Get out of here!"

1 "I dunno who dunnit."

2 "I wanna be a pop star."

3 "Who's gonna tell her?"

4 "I've gotta go now."

5 "Are you alright?"

(Answers: page 193)

Starting and finishing a sentence

a A sentence is a group of words that makes complete sense. There is only one way of starting a sentence. The first word of a sentence must begin with a capital letter.

b A full stop is used to mark the end of a sentence – except when you are asking a direct question (?) or making an exclamation (!).

   e.g. Does anybody know where Shefali is?

       What a nuisance!

Of all the punctuation marks, the full stop is the most important. Just as a red traffic-light stops one line of traffic from crashing into another, so too the full stop prevents one sentence from running into the next. It stops one set of words from becoming confused with another.

c The exclamation mark (!) is a very 'loud' punctuation mark. We use it to express very strong emotions (like anger, shock, pleasure or amazement).

   e.g. What a stupid thing to say!

Correct the advertisement below. Each sentence should start with a capital letter. Each sentence should end with a full stop.

come and enjoy a relaxing holiday at the Dolphin Hotel it is very near a clean beach and there are plenty of shops nearby the hotel is situated in a quiet area and has its own large swimming pool

the rooms are spacious and clean, and each one has its own private bath and shower with hot and cold water there is a colour TV in each room and a telephone if you want to call room service

our staff are friendly and we offer a high level of service you will find everybody helpful and cheerful there is always someone at the reception desk to help you with any problems

the hotel has two lifts there is a lounge with comfortable armchairs and a wide selection of newspapers and magazines

(Answers: page 193)

45 Suffixes

a We can extend a word by adding a suffix. Note what happens to words of one syllable when we add the following suffixes: *-ing*, *-ish*, *-ed*, *-er*, *-est*, *-en*.

- The final consonant is doubled if the base word has one vowel followed by one consonant.
  e.g. sit – sitting; fat – fatter; mad – madden; rub – rubbed; dim – dimmed; red – reddish

  Exceptions: The letters *w*, *x* and *y* are never doubled.
  e.g. row – rowing; tax – taxed; play – played

- The final consonant is not doubled if the base word has two vowels followed by one consonant.
  e.g. steer – steering; hear – hearing; heat – heated; wood – wooden

  Exception: wool – woollen

- If the base word ends in *-e*, the preceding consonant is not usually doubled.
  e.g. hope – hoped; phone – phoned; shine – shining; fine – finest

  Don't forget *-e* disappears in front of a suffix beginning with *-i*.
  e.g. smile – smiling; take – taking; blue – bluish

- With words ending in a consonant + *-y*, the *-y* changes to *-i* when we add *-er*, *-est* or *-ed*.
  e.g. cry – cried; dry – drier; trendy – trendiest

b Whenever you are in doubt as to whether to double a letter or to keep it single, apply the following pronunciation rule:
one consonant follows a <u>long</u> vowel sound;
two consonants follow a <u>short</u> vowel sound.
e.g. later – the latter; hoping (hope) – hopping (hop); writing – written; biting – bitter – bitten; dining room – dinner-time

c Many suffixes begin with a vowel: **e.g.** *-ed, -er, -ee, -ing, -ation, -able, -ence.* If we add any of these suffixes to a word of more than one syllable ending in one vowel + *-l*, the *-l* will double.

    e.g. quarrel – quarrelled – quarrelling;
             cancel – cancelled – cancelling

The letter *-l* does not double, however, if there are two vowels in front.

    e.g. conceal – concealed; reveal – revealing

d For all other words of more than one syllable ending in one vowel + consonant, we should apply the following rules:

- If the stress in pronunciation falls on the last syllable, then the final consonant is doubled if we add a suffix beginning with a vowel.
  e.g. regret – regretted – regrettable; begin – beginning

- If the stress does not fall on the last syllable, then the final consonant is not doubled.
  e.g. offer – offered; develop – developed; benefit – benefiting

- It is with words like *prefer* and *refer* that the stress rule is particularly important.
  e.g. prefer – preferred – preferring *but* preference – preferably
         refer – referred *but* reference

  Exceptions: handicap – handicapped; worship – worshipped – worshipping; kidnap – kidnapper – kidnapping (The *-p* is doubled in these three words though the stress does not fall on the last syllable.)

e Note very carefully that the final consonant is not doubled if the suffix begins with a consonant.
  e.g. fulfilment, commitment, quarrelsome

f Note that *-c* becomes *-ck* in words such as *panic* and *mimic.*
  e.g. panicked, mimicked

g When a verb ends in *-qui* + consonant, we treat the *-ui* as a single vowel and apply the normal stress rules.
  e.g. acquit – acquitted; equip – equipped

I   Extend each verb in brackets with the suffix at the end of the sentence.

1   What's (happen)? (-*ing*)

2   He left because he did not find the job very (fulfil). (-*ing*)

3   The kitchen is (equip) with all the latest gadgets. (-*ed*)

4   We need to buy some more (equip). (-*ment*)

5   The first (instal) is due in February. (-*ment*)

II Add -*ing* or -*ed* to the words in brackets and make any other necessary changes.

1   He has to be on the (win) side. He hates being on the (lose) side.

2   We (wait) until he had (cool) down, and then we (beg) him not to leave.

3   We are (write) to inform you that we are (plan) to take over your company.

4   I was (hope) he'd be in a better mood this afternoon, but he is (hop) mad!

5   He (try) to hold it tight, but it (slip) out of his hand.

6   Please stop (tap) your feet. And please stop (bite) your nails!

7   The little child (yawn) and (rub) his sleepy eyes.

(Answers: page 193)

46　Tricky verbs

a　*lay* and *lie*

(see Unit 30 'h')

b　*raise* and *rise*
- *Raise* is a transitive verb. It requires an object.
  e.g.　She raised *her voice.*

- *Rise* is an intransitive verb. It does not take an object.
  e.g.　Her voice rose in anger.

c　*teach* and *learn*
You *learn to do* something, but someone *teaches you to do* something.

d　*hung* and *hanged*
We use *hanged* as the past form of *hang* when we are referring to someone being killed by means of hanging. In all other cases, we use *hung* as the past form of *hang*.

e　*was* and *were*
- In written English we use *I*, *he*, *she*, *it* + <u>was</u>; and *we*, *you*, *they* + <u>were</u>.

- The only exception to the above is when we create *imaginary* situations with *if* and *wish*.
  e.g.　If only he were here. / I wish I were rich. / If I were you, I'd say nothing.

f　*doesn't* and *don't*
Without exception, we use *he*, *she*, *it* + <u>doesn't</u>; and *I*, *we*, *you*, *they* + <u>don't</u>.

Underline the correct alternative in brackets.

1   My mother told me to (lie / lay) down and get some sleep.

2   Our hens haven't (lain / laid) any eggs for days.

3   They have (raised / risen) his salary by 10 per cent.

4   His salary has (raised / risen) by 10 per cent.

5   My father is (teaching / learning) me to drive.

6   She (hung / hanged) the washing out on the line.

7   They (was / were) pleased to see us.

8   I wouldn't do that if I (was / were) you.

9   If she (doesn't / don't) behave, she will be punished.

(Answers: page 193)

47 Unnecessary words

a In spoken English, we use various devices to emphasise a word or phrase. One way of emphasising a point is to use different vocabulary to say the same thing twice.

e.g. It was the right and proper thing to do.

A word or phrase which merely repeats the sense of a word or phrase that has just been used is a 'tautology' (unnecessary and usually unintentional repetition). In written English, the unnecessary repetition of a word or phrase should be avoided.

Over the years, various tautological expressions have crept into the English language and have become part of our normal vocabulary.

e.g. null and void; prim and proper; peace and quiet

These are, however, fixed phrases. In your own writing, you should not create phrases of this type.

b A common error in written English is to confuse a two-part verb with a verb that is complete in itself.

e.g. We returned back to the hotel.

✓ We <u>went back</u> to the hotel.

✓ We <u>returned</u> to the hotel.

c Be careful not to use superfluous 'ornaments' in written English.

e.g. Past experience has taught me that one should not judge people by their appearance.

Since *experience* in this sentence clearly relates to the past, the word *past* is redundant.

d Look at the following two sentences:

i I was speaking in jest, but he took my words literally and was quite upset.

ii My brother dashed out of the house and literally flew down the road.

- The first sentence would not make sense without the adverb *literally*. In the second sentence, however, *literally* does not make sense as the verb *flew* is clearly being used in an imaginative or metaphorical way.

- The use of *literally* in the second sentence is an example of a common device used in spoken English. When employing *figurative* (imaginative / metaphorical) speech, we often use *literally* as an 'intensifier'. An intensifier is an adverb or adjective which adds emphasis to the word or phrase which follows it.
  e.g. I am <u>very</u> happy.

Although common in spoken English, the use of *literally* as an intensifier should be avoided in written English.

- The adjective *actual* is another word that is often used as an intensifier in spoken English.
  e.g. This is the actual dress worn by my grandmother when she got married.

Since *actual* means *real* or *current / present*, the word clearly has no meaning in the example above. This use of *actual* should be avoided in written English.

Cross out any unnecessary words in the sentences below.

1 We were surrounded on all sides by thick, dense vegetation.

2 The atrocious weather was so awful that we decided to return back home.

3 He was unemployed and out of work for a period of three months.

4 Each and every student will receive a free complimentary copy of the magazine.

5 Despite his lack of experience, nevertheless he was offered the job.

6 Past experience has taught me not to mix business with pleasure.

7 As soon as you get home, please phone me immediately.

8 It was an issue that divided and split the Socialist Party.

9 It was not until ten years later that scientists appreciated the importance and significance of the discovery.

10 Her eyes literally shone like diamonds.

(Answers: page 194)

48 Word endings 1: -*ible* and -*able*

a With or without *e*?

You will never find *e* in front of -*ible*.

We normally drop the *e* in front of -*able*.
e.g. adore – adorable; advise – advisable; forgive – forgivable

 Exceptions: • We usually keep the *e* with words that end in -*ce* or -*ge*.
      e.g. notice – noticeable; knowledge – knowledgeable; change – changeable

      • We keep the *e* if the word ends in -*ee*.
      e.g. agree – agreeable; foresee – foreseeable

      • In theory, we should drop the *e* when adding -*able* to the following words: *like, love, live, move, size*. In practice, it is entirely up to you whether to keep or drop the *e*. Thus: like – likable / likeable; love – lovable / loveable; live – livable / liveable; move – movable / moveable; size – sizable / sizeable.

b Single or double consonant?

Note carefully the spelling of the following words:
    forget   + -*able* = *forgettable*
    regret   + -*able* = *regrettable*
    prefer   + -*able* = *preferable*
    transfer + -*able* = *transferable*

c -*ible* or -*able*?

There is no easy way of distinguishing between words ending in -*ible* and -*able*. You may, however, find the following guidelines useful:

  • The vast majority of words will end in -*able*. Treat those that end in -*ible* as exceptions.

- Base words that are complete (or almost complete) in themselves tend to take -*able*.
  e.g. accept – acceptable; avoid – avoidable

- Words that can take the suffix -*ion* will very often take -*ible*.
  e.g. divide – division – divisible; vision – visible; comprehension – comprehensible

- Very often -*ible* follows -*s*.
  e.g. sensible, possible, responsible

- Never place -*ible* after a vowel.
  e.g. reliable, viable, sociable

TASK

Where a word is incomplete, complete it with either -*ible* or -*able*.

1 The heat was unbear _____ .

2 He is very soci _____ .

3 No army is invinc _____ .

4 The word *dinosaur* actually means 'terr _____ lizard'.

5 They said it was imposs _____ to do that.

6 The delay was unavoid _____ .

7 The food was horr _____ . In fact, it was ined _____ .

8 Be careful. That material is inflamm _____ .

9 His writing is illeg _____ .

(Answers: page 194)

Word endings 2: *-ent* and *-ant*

a Certain words may end in *-ent* or *-ant*.

- (in)dependent (an adjective); a dependant (a noun)
- a currant (a fruit); a current (a flow of air / water / electricity); the current climate (*current* = 'of the present time')

b Apart from the examples given above and a few other words, it is not easy to distinguish between *-ent* and *-ant* because they invariably sound the same, and either ending can denote a noun or an adjective.

c It is best to learn the most common words by heart as you come across them. It is, however, well worth knowing a few rules of thumb concerning the use of *-ent* and *-ant*:

- A noun that describes what somebody does in terms of a job or a trade will usually end in *-ant*.
  e.g. assistant, attendant, accountant, servant

  On the other hand, if the noun has a soft *g*, it will end in *-ent*.
  e.g. agent, regent

- The last point mentioned above also applies to adjectives. A soft *g* tells us the ending will be *-ent*, and a hard *g* tells us that the ending will be *-ant*.
  e.g. diligent, intelligent *but*
  elegant, arrogant, extravagant

- Likewise, *-ent* will follow a soft *c*, and *-ant* will follow a hard *c*.
  e.g. decent, recent *but*
  significant, vacant

- *-ent* usually follows certain letter combinations:

  - *-cid-*, *-fid-*, *-sid-*, *-vid-*
    e.g. incident, confident, resident, president, evident

  - *-flu-*, *-qu-*
    e.g. fluent, frequent

  - *-sist-*
    e.g. consistent, insistent

    Exceptions: assistant, resistant

| TASK |

Where a word is incomplete, complete it with either *-ent* or *-ant*.

1 I hate feeling depend _____ on others.

2 He said that his elderly mother was his only
   depend _____ .

3 Australia is an independ _____ nation.

4 She claims to be a direct descend _____ of Queen Victoria.

5 He said he was not interested in curr _____ affairs.

6 A cloakroom attend _____ took my coat.

7 That's not relev _____ to our discussion!

8 She was most insist _____ on that point.

9 How did the accid _____ happen?

10 He doesn't sound very confid _____ .

11 He is extremely arrog _____ .

12 This material is fire-resist _____ .

13 There has been a signific _____ increase in burglaries.

14 She is flu _____ in five languages.

(Answers: page 194)

There are no hard and fast rules to help you decide whether a word should end in -*ary*, -*ery*, -*ory* or -*ury*. There are, however, a few rules of thumb that are worth bearing in mind.

a It's often possible to work out the spelling of a word by thinking of a word related to it.

    e.g. burglar – burglary; robber – robbery; director – directory; injure – injury

b Words ending in -*ery* are usually nouns.

    e.g. cemetery, stationery, machinery

     Exceptions: slippery, fiery, watery

c Nouns ending in -*ery* often contain a complete smaller word within them.

    e.g. (deliver)y; (scene)ry; (green)ery; (adult)ery

d Very few words end in -*ury*, and they are usually nouns.

    e.g. century, fury, injury, jury, mercury, perjury, treasury

     Exception: bury

e Words ending in -*ary* or -*ory* may be adjectives or nouns.

    e.g. Adjectives (-*ary*):
        customary, necessary, stationary (= not moving), voluntary
        Nouns (-*ary*):
        anniversary, dictionary, library, salary
        Adjectives (-*ory*):
        advisory, compulsory, extrasensory, obligatory
        Nouns (-*ory*):
        category, dormitory, factory, history, memory

Where a word is incomplete, add one of the following endings: *-ary*, *-ery*, *-ory*, *-ury*.

1 There was an explosion in the laborat _____ .

2 The torch needs a new batt _____ .

3 She needs to widen her vocabul _____ .

4 He was awarded a medal for brav _____ .

5 The car skidded on the slipp _____ road.

6 It wasn't a serious inj _____ .

7 The soldier was arrested by the milit _____ police.

8 Tom's brother is a mission _____ in Africa.

9 Would you spend a night alone in a cemet _____ ?

10 I couldn't find his number in the telephone direct _____ .

(Answers: page 194)

51 Word endings 4: *-us, -ous, -ious, -eous*

a Words that end in *-us* tend to be <u>nouns</u> of Latin origin.
   e.g. cactus, fungus, nucleus, opus, radius, stimulus, terminus

Words that end in *-ous, -ious* and *-eous* tend to be <u>adjectives</u>.

b To avoid confusing *-eous* with *-ious*, it is best to learn by heart the most common adjectives ending in *-eous*.
   e.g. advantageous, courageous, courteous, erroneous, gorgeous, hideous, instantaneous, miscellaneous, nauseous, outrageous, simultaneous, spontaneous

You should also be aware of the most common adjectives that end in *-ious*, but where the *i* sounds like *e*.
   e.g. curious, delirious, hilarious, laborious, notorious, previous, serious

c To avoid confusing *-ous* with *-ious*, you should note that the letter *t*, *c* and *x* combine with *-ious* to give us a *sh* sound.
   e.g. ambitious, anxious, conscientious, conscious, delicious, ferocious, luscious, obnoxious, pretentious, spacious, superstitious

d Note that the stem changes when *-ous* is added to the following words:
   • grief – grievous; mischief – mischievous
   • humour – humorous; rigour – rigorous; vigour – vigorous
   • disaster – disastrous; monster – monstrous

e Note that an *-ious* ending may be the result of a *y* changing to *i* when *-ous* is added.
   e.g. envy – envious / fury – furious / mystery – mysterious / vary – various

f Sometimes *u* is placed before *-ous*.
   e.g. ambiguous, conspicuous, promiscuous

g In most other cases when deciding between *-ous* and *-ious*, the sound of the word should indicate whether an *i* is necessary.
   e.g. adventurous, pompous, tedious

| TASK |

Where a word is incomplete, add *-us*, *-ous*, *-ious* or *-eous*.

1 He was attacked by a feroc _____ dog.

2 Your daughter has a vir _____ and should stay in bed.

3 He is a notor _____ criminal.

4 It was a spontan _____ decision.

5 What a ludicr _____ thing to say!

6 She felt quite self-consc _____ .

7 His spelling is atroc _____ .

8 Her son is very ambit _____ .

(Answers: page 194)

124

Words 1: one word or maybe / may be two?

a Look carefully at the words underlined below. Where one word is used, note the explanation in brackets. Where two words have been used, this means that they are two separate words of equal value. In each case, the grammar of the sentence tells us whether to use one word or two.

- They have <u>already</u> gone. (an adverb)
  They are <u>all</u> <u>ready</u> to carry out your orders.

- I was not <u>altogether</u> satisfied with her reply. (= entirely)
  I would prefer to see them <u>all</u> <u>together</u>, not separately.

- <u>Anyone</u> could have taken it. (= anybody)
  <u>Any</u> <u>one</u> of those students could have taken it.

- Is <u>everyone</u> here? (= everybody)
  Look at these sentences. <u>Every</u> <u>one</u> of them is wrong.

- Burglary is an <u>everyday</u> occurrence. (an adjective)
  I go jogging <u>every</u> <u>day</u>.

- <u>Maybe</u> I ought to tell the police. (= perhaps)
  They <u>may be</u> in Australia. (modal verb + main verb)

- <u>Anyway</u>, what does it matter? (= anyhow)
  Is there <u>any way</u> of raising more money before the deadline?

- I didn't even get a <u>thank-you</u>. (*or* thankyou) (a noun)
  I sent her a <u>thank-you</u> (*or* thankyou) letter. (an adjective)
  <u>Thank you</u> very much for what you've done.

b The negative form of *can* is *can't* or *cannot* (one word).

c The following are written as two words: *no one* (= nobody); *in case*;
   a lot; *in front*; *as well*.

d Be careful not to confuse a compound noun (e.g. a goldfish) with
   an adjective and noun (e.g. a gold fish = a fish made of gold).

TASK

Underline the correct alternative in brackets.

1 (Thankyou / Thank you) for your help.

2 I have (all ready / already) seen that film.

3 They were (all ready / already) and waiting when I arrived.

4 That will be £23 (altogether / all together).

5 Has (any one / anyone) seen my blue sweater?

6 When the alarm went off, (everyone / every one) panicked.

7 I see her (everyday / every day).

8 I (maybe / may be) late tomorrow.

(Answers: page 194)

53 Words 2: two words in one

a When a word ends in *-ll*, it usually loses one *l* when it is joined to another word.

    e.g. all + most = almost; well + come = welcome; power + full = powerful; care + full = careful; beauty + full = beautiful

(Note that consonant *+-y* becomes consonant *+-i* when joined to *full*.)

b When two words ending in *-ll* are joined together, they both lose one *l*.

    e.g. skill + full = skilful; full + fill = fulfil; will + full = wilful

c Do not confuse adjectives with adverbs. To form an adverb, one usually adds *-ly* to an adjective. Accordingly, adjectives that end in *-ful* will end in *-fully* when they become adverbs.

    e.g. painful – painfully; cheerful – cheerfully

d If two words are joined by a hyphen, a word ending in *-ll* does not change to a single *l*.

    e.g. well-off, well-known, all-out, all-round, full-time, ill-advised

You should also note that *-ll* is retained in certain 'compound' words. A *compound word* is a word formed from other words.

    e.g. overall, farewell, fullback

e When two words are put together to make a compound word, the words usually remain complete.

    e.g. with + hold = withhold; grand + daughter = granddaughter; over + rate = overrate; pass + word = password

 Exceptions: grand + dad = grandad *or* granddad; pass + time = pastime

If in doubt when joining two words, use a hyphen.

    e.g. earring or ear-ring

Complete each sentence with the correct form of the word in brackets.

e.g. We had a _____ time. (wonder) → wonderful

1 He was a _____ king and forgave her. (mercy)

2 I hope you will be _____ . (succeed)

3 What a _____ baby! (beauty)

4 We felt sorry for him: he looked so _____ . (pity)

5 Please be more _____ in future. (care)

(Answers: page 195)

Appendix 1

Confusing words 1

Words that look alike are a major source of confusion when reading or writing. Whenever in doubt, check the meaning and spelling of the word in a dictionary. Note carefully the dictionary meanings of the following words:

a   to affect = to produce an effect on / to make a difference to; an effect = result / consequence; to effect (e.g. a change) = to bring about / to accomplish / to put into effect

b   averse (to) = opposed (to); adverse = negative / hostile

c   allusion = reference; illusion = deception / delusion

d   appreciative = showing one's appreciation; appreciable = considerable / noticeable

e   to compliment = to praise; to complement = to complete / to combine well with

f   corps = select group; corpse = dead body

g   to envelop = to wrap up in / to cover closely on all sides; an envelope = used for sending letters

h   eminent = distinguished / famous; imminent = soon to happen

i   to elicit = to draw out; illicit = illegal

j   to elude = to avoid / to escape; to allude (to) = to refer (to)

k   an enquiry = a general request for information; an inquiry = an official investigation

1 <u>explicit</u> = clear / definite / open; <u>implicit</u> = implied (but not openly expressed)

m <u>human</u> = relating to (or concerning) people; <u>humane</u> = kind / not cruel / merciful

n <u>ingenious</u> = original / brilliant; <u>ingenuous</u> = innocent / naive

TASK

Complete each statement or question by underlining the correct alternative in brackets.

1 It made no difference. It didn't (affect / effect) us at all.

2 It was just an optical (allusion / illusion).

3 It was quite an (appreciative / appreciable) rise in price.

4 I'd like to (compliment / complement) you on your work.

5 Have you got a spare (envelop / envelope)?

6 Many (eminent / imminent) scientists agree with her.

7 Who will stop the (elicit / illicit) trade in whale meat?

8 The escaped prisoner (eluded / alluded) capture for over a week.

9 There was an official (inquiry / enquiry) into the disaster.

10 He is brilliant. He has come up with an (ingenious / ingenuous) solution to the problem.

(Answers: page 195)

Confusing words 2

Note carefully the following:

a to imply = to hint (to state something indirectly); to infer = to deduce (to draw a conclusion from what has been stated)

b morale = a general feeling of confidence / enthusiasm / determination; moral (adjective) = relating to standards of good or bad behaviour / fairness / honesty, etc.

c respectfully = politely; respectively = in the order stated

d especially = in particular; specially = something done for a particular purpose

e access = means of approaching or entering a place / opportunity to use or approach somebody or something; excess = too much of something

f stationery (noun) = paper, envelopes, things for writing; stationary (adjective) = not moving

g regrettable = to be regretted / describing something one regrets (e.g. a regrettable mistake); regretful = feeling or expressing regret (e.g. a regretful shake of the head)

h principal (adjective) = main / chief / primary; principle (noun) = a basic idea / belief / doctrine; in principle = in theory

i loath (or loth) = unwilling / reluctant; to loathe = to detest / to hate

j uninterested = indifferent / not interested; disinterested = impartial / unbiased

k later = the comparative form of *late*; the latter = the second of two people or things already mentioned

As you read the text below, underline the correct alternative in brackets.

"Am I to (infer / imply) from what you are saying that you are dissatisfied with the way we manage things here?" asked Mr Rosinger in an icy tone.

"All I am saying is that (moral / morale) amongst staff is very low," replied Mr Atkins. "I merely wish to point out, most (respectfully / respectively), that we are all rather concerned about the lack of communication between management and staff – (especially / specially) with regard to certain changes in the office. For instance, we no longer have free (access / excess) to the (stationery / stationary) cupboard. Nobody, however, has told us why. This breakdown in communication is most (regrettable / regretful) and we feel that something must be done about it."

Mr Rosinger grunted, blew three rings of cigar smoke into the air and then asked very quietly:

"Is that your (principal / principle) grievance, Mr Atkins?"

"Of course not. However, I am (loath / loathe) to discuss this matter any further without other members of staff being present. Could we not arrange for a formal meeting to take place between management and staff, perhaps with someone (disinterested / uninterested) in the chair?"

Mr Rosinger chewed slowly on his cigar.

"Would you like my reply now or (later / latter)?" he drawled.

"Now, please."

"(You're / Your) fired!"

(Answers: page 195)

Confusing words 3

Note carefully the following pairs of words and their meanings:

a   flair = natural ability / talent; flare = (a) a bright light or flame, (b) a device that produces bright light or coloured smoke

b   to afflict = to cause someone physical or mental suffering (Something afflicts you or you are afflicted with something.)

   to inflict something on someone = to make someone suffer / experience something unpleasant / to impose something unpleasant on someone

c   to broach a subject = to raise a matter / bring up a point for discussion; a brooch = an ornament worn on clothes

d   to emigrate = to go and live in another country; to immigrate = to come into a country in order to live there

e   with bated breath = anxiously / excitedly; baited (past form of *to bait*) (a) to bait a person / animal means to harass / pester / annoy / tease the person or animal intentionally, (b) to bait a hook with a worm means to place a worm on a hook in order to catch a fish

f   to flout = deliberately to disobey (someone or something) in an open and defiant manner; to flaunt = to exhibit something in such a way that everybody is forced to take notice of it

g   filing = related to *file*; filling = related to *fill*

h   some time = a little time / an amount of time; sometime = (a) at some point of time, (b) formerly

i   luxurious = related to luxury (expensive / opulent / extremely comfortable); luxuriant = related to healthy growth (thick, lush)

j   heroin = an addictive drug; heroine = female equivalent of *hero*

k Sometimes, the verbs 'leave' and 'forget' have the same idea but are used slightly differently.

    e.g. 'Oh no, I have forgotten my passport. (correct)
        'Oh no, I have forgotten my passport *in the hotel room*.' (wrong)
        'Oh no, I have *left* my passport *in the hotel*.' (correct)

TASK

Underline the correct alternative in brackets.

1 She has a (flare / flair) for languages.

2 Rheumatism (inflicts / afflicts) both the young and the old.

3 Be careful how you (broach / brooch) the subject with him.

4 My best friend has decided to leave Ireland and (emigrate / immigrate) to Australia.

5 We waited for the result with (baited / bated) breath.

6 If he persists in (flouting / flaunting) all our rules and regulations, we shall have to expel him from school.

7 Make sure you lock the (filing / filling) cabinet.

8 I am sure that I will see her (some time / sometime) this week.

9 They discovered that she was a (heroin / heroine) addict.

10 The hotel was surrounded by (luxurious / luxuriant) tropical vegetation.

(Answers: page 195)

Confusing words 4

Note carefully the following:

a   authoritative = commanding respect; authoritarian = demanding obedience

b   emotive = arousing strong emotions; emotional = showing emotion / centred on emotion

c   definite = clear / certain / fixed; definitive = (a) not likely to be improved upon, (b) final / best / most authoritative

d   odious = disgusting / hateful; odorous = related to odour (smell)

e   erotic = relating to / arousing sexual desire; exotic = related to tropical countries / unusual and exciting

f   contemptible = deserving contempt; contemptuous = showing contempt

g   deceased = (recently) dead; diseased = infected

h   efficient = working / operating properly and in an organised way; effective = achieving / producing the desired effect

i   deficient = lacking something / not as good as it should be; defective = (a) having a defect / defects, (b) imperfect / incomplete

j   urban = related to city / town; urbane = civilised / confident / refined / well-mannered

k   blond = fair (masculine); blonde = fair (feminine)

When describing hair, either *blond* or *blonde* can be used for either gender.

l   quite = fairly, rather; quiet = not noisy

m   a desert = a waterless, treeless region; to desert = to abandon; dessert = pudding / sweet

n a serial = a single story presented in separate instalments;
a series = a set of different stories with the same characters

o unaware = ignorant of / not conscious of; unawares = by surprise

> *Note:* Strangely enough, flammable and inflammable have the
> same meaning (capable of catching fire). The opposite is non-
> flammable.

TASK

Underline the correct alternative in brackets.

1 His manner was so (authoritative / authoritarian) that we were too
scared to ask questions.

2 Capital punishment is a highly (emotive / emotional) issue.

3 It is every academic's dream to write the (definite / definitive)
book on his or her subject.

4 Comparisons are (odious / odorous).

5 That was a (contemptible / contemptuous) thing to do! You ought
to be ashamed of yourself.

6 The families of the (diseased / deceased) are demanding an official
inquiry into the circumstances surrounding the air crash.

7 She still hasn't found an (effective / efficient) remedy for her
migraines.

8 Junk food is usually (deficient / defective) in vitamins and vital
minerals.

9 He finds (urban / urbane) life too stressful and is hoping to move
to the country.

10 We were (quite / quiet) happy to have just a banana for (desert /
dessert).

(Answers: page 195)

Appendix 2

Words ending in *-k, -ck* and *-ke*

a At the end of a word you may find either *-ke* or *-ck*. The sound of the word should help you to choose the correct ending.
  e.g. *-ke*: snake, bake, like, lake, sake, rake, bike, broke
       -ck: snack, back, lick, lack, sack, rack, brick, black

b At the end of a word, you may find *-k* or *-ck*.

  • The letter *-k* follows <u>two</u> vowels:
    e.g. look, shook, break, book, week, weak, cheek, meek, leak, creak

  • The letter *-k* follows a vowel + <u>consonant</u>:
    e.g. thank, trunk, sink, ask, task, risk

  • The letters *-ck* follow a <u>single</u> vowel:
    e.g. lock, sock, track, trick, check, crack, neck, struck, knock

  > *Note:* The letters *-ck* are also found in the middle of a word.
  > The same rule applies: *-ck* is found after a single vowel.
  > e.g. stocking, chicken, pocket, racket, rocket, bucket, jacket

c Once you know the spelling of a short word, remember that *-k* or *-ck* will not change when you make it into a longer word.
  e.g. like – liked – liking; lick – licked – licking; knock – knocked – knocking; risk – risky; luck – lucky; break – breakfast; pack – packed – package – packet

In each sentence there is an incomplete word. Complete the word with
-ke or *-ck* so that the sentence makes sense.

1 We weren't very hungry, so we just had a sna_____ .

2 She screamed when she saw the sna_____ .

3 Don't li_____ your plate!

4 I've hurt my ba_____ .

5 We're going to ba_____ some potatoes.

(Answers: page 195)

Appendix 3

Some problems of usage

There are many pairs or groups of words in the English language which closely resemble one another in appearance or meaning, and consequently are confusing. Now carefully study the following list:

a   The word *number* implies a group of separate items.
   e.g.   a number of students / chairs / pens

   The word *amount* implies a mass and is used with 'uncountable' nouns.
   e.g.   a particular amount of time / work / sugar / flour

b   beside = next to; *besides* = in addition to, apart from

c   personal = private; *personnel* = staff in a company or business

d   imaginary = not real; *imaginative* = showing great imagination

e   historic = important, significant in history (e.g. a historic moment / building); *historical* = concerning past events
   (e.g. historical research / facts)

f   economical = not expensive / not wasteful; *economic* = to do with the economy (e.g. the government's economic policy)

g   electric = powered by electricity (e.g. an electric fire / cooker / heater); *electrical* = a general adjective (e.g. an electrical engineer / appliance / fault)

h   classic = of particularly high quality / a good example of its kind (e.g. This record is a classic.), very typical (e.g. a classic example / mistake); *classical* = serious and traditional in style (e.g. classical music)

i <u>continual</u> = describes something that happens repeatedly;
<u>continuous</u> = unbroken, without interruption

(see also Appendix 1 *Confusing Words*)

TASK

I **Underline the correct alternative in brackets.**

  1 I was surprised at the (amount / number) of mistakes he made.

  2 She does not have the right qualifications for the job,
       (beside / besides) which she is far too young.

  3 I was interviewed by the (personal / personnel) manager.

  4 He is a very (imaginary / imaginative) writer.

  5 She is studying (classical / classic) and modern ballet.

(Answers: page 195)

Knowledge check

Adjectives

I There is at least one spelling mistake in each of the following sentences. Underline and correct each mistake.

1 I was feeling hungrey and thirsty.

2 She got angrey with me and said some really horible things.

3 Although the weather was awfull, we had a wonderfull holiday.

4 I've got short wavey hair and rosey cheeks.

5 My brother's got long straite hair.

6 I'm usually cheerfull and easygoing, but I have a nastey temper.

7 My brother's quite shy and doesn't like noisey parties.

8 The stoney path was really ruff on our feet and I was quite glad when we reached the grassy hillside.

9 It was dificult to tell whether I had a cold or flu. I had a runy nose and a terible cough. On the other hand, my temperature was normal.

10 The food was tastey.

11 That's not posible, is it?

12 The operation was painfull but necesery.

Score: /20

II 1 Complete each adjective below with *in-* or *un-*.

an _____ efficient secretary; an _____ even surface; an _____ grateful child; an _____ expensive present; an _____ convenient moment; an _____ fair decision; an _____ curable disease; an _____ accurate answer; an _____ formal interview; an _____ usual colour

Score: /10

2 Complete each adjective below with *im-* or *un-*.

an _____ polite remark; an _____ popular decision; an _____ pleasant sight; an _____ patient teacher

Score: /4

3 Complete each adjective below with *ir-*, *il-* or *un-*.

_____ responsible parents; an _____ reliable worker; _____ legible handwriting; an _____ reasonable request; _____ lucky numbers; an _____ literate peasant

Score: /6

4 Complete each adjective below with *dis-* or *un-*.

_____ obedient children; _____ satisfactory work; _____ respectful students; _____ loyal workers; _____ fortunate results

Score: /5

III Decide whether each adjective in brackets should end in *-er* or *-est*. Write out each adjective.

1 The Moon is much (small) and (light) than the Earth.

2 Some of the world's (big) mountains are on the seabed. Some undersea mountains are (tall) than those on land.

3 Some seas are (salty) than others. The Dead Sea, between Jordan and Israel, is so salty that no fish can live in it.

4 As you climb up a mountain, the air becomes (thin) and it becomes (hard) to breathe. That's why mountaineers carry extra oxygen with them.

5 More than 120 million people cross the border between Mexico and the USA every year, making it the (busy) frontier in the world.

6 Deserts are the (hot) and (dry) places on Earth. The Antarctic is the (cold) and (windy) place in the world.

7 The (wide) road in the world is the Monumental Axis in Brasilia, Brazil. It is 250 metres wide, which is wide enough for 160 cars parked side by side.

8 The Arctic is the (small) of the oceans, and the Pacific is the (large).

Score: /15
(Answers: page 196)

Adverbs

I Complete each sentence by forming an adverb from the adjective in brackets.

1 The doctor saw me _____ . (immediate)

2 She reacted _____ to the news. (angry)

3 He _____ set fire to her dress. (accidental)

4 He is _____ strong. (incredible)

5 It's _____ cheap! (fantastic)

6 The building was _____ destroyed in the fire. (complete)

7 He _____ doesn't want to see you. (probable)

8 She _____ needed some help. (desperate)

9 She is _____ upset. (terrible)

10 Could you _____ come in earlier tomorrow? (possible)

11 We _____ have fish for supper on Fridays. (usual)

12 _____ we heard a scream. (sudden)

13 They are _____ married. (happy)

14 _____ , he is not well. (unfortunate)

15 She's _____ on time. (normal)

Score: /15

II Using the underlined words as the basis for your answer, rephrase each sentence below without changing its meaning. Each sentence should contain an adverb. Start your sentence as indicated in brackets.

e.g. He was <u>foolish</u> enough <u>to believe</u> everything he read in the papers.
(He ...) = He foolishly believed everything he read in the papers.

1 His <u>response</u> to her request was <u>sympathetic</u>.

He _____

2 They have the <u>occasional argument</u>, like all couples.

They _____

3 He demanded their <u>unconditional surrender</u>.

He said that they had to _____

4 Her <u>behaviour</u> was <u>unpredictable</u>.

She _____

5 My <u>original plan</u> was to have a very quiet wedding.

I had _____

6 His proposal came in for <u>heavy criticism</u> from everybody concerned.

His proposal was _____

7 Their <u>struggle</u> against impossible odds was <u>heroic</u>.

They _____

8 His <u>injuries</u> were <u>fatal</u>.

He was _____

9 The <u>probable cause</u> of the fire was an electrical fault.

The fire was _____

10 Her <u>death</u> was <u>peaceful</u>.

She _____

11 There has been a <u>dramatic rise</u> in the cost of petrol.

The cost of petrol has _____

12 The <u>suffering</u> they endured was <u>terrible</u>.

They _____

13 It was very <u>sensible</u> of her <u>to call</u> the police.

She _____

14 He gave her an <u>angry look</u>.

He _____

15 Despite his <u>profuse apologies</u>, she would not forgive him.

Although he _____

Score: /15

(Answers: page 196)

American and British spelling

Underline and change any examples of American spelling in the sentences below.

1   She dialed the wrong number.

2   He didn't have a beard, but he had a mustache.

3   They spent two weeks analyzing the data.

4   There's a draft in here. Could you close the window?

5   Has anybody seen my pajamas?

6   He bought her some jewelry for her birthday.

7   Jaimini's father is a famous archeologist.

8   They are paying for the carpet by installments.

9   We went for a walk thru the forest.

10   He was admitted to hospital with a brain hemorrhage.

11   On his second attempt, he equaled the world record.

12   We were rather skeptical about their chances of winning the match.

Score: /12

(Answers: page 197)

Apostrophes 1: to show omission

I   Read the following jokes. Five of the words need an apostrophe. Decide where the apostrophes should be placed.

Jane: What follows a dog everywhere?
Ali: I dont know.
Jane: Its tail!

Gary: Im glad I wasnt born in France.
Mike: Why?
Gary: I cant speak French.

Score: /5

II   Shorten the words that have been underlined.

e.g.   I think <u>she is</u> away ➔ she's

1   She <u>does not</u> look well.

2   <u>They are</u> late again.

146

3   <u>That is</u> my dad over there.

4   <u>There is</u> someone at the door.

5   It looks as if <u>it is</u> going to rain.

6   <u>Who has</u> taken my jacket?

7   <u>I have</u> done my homework.

8   <u>She has</u> been absent for the past two weeks.

9   We <u>were not</u> told the truth.

10   You <u>should not</u> do that.

Score: /10
(Answers: page 197)

Apostrophes 2: to show possession

I   Place apostrophes where appropriate in the sentences below.

1   Theyve gone off to Rome for a fortnights holiday.

2   They said theyd see us in two weeks time.

3   We took Mrs Browns dog to the vets this morning.

4   Heres the ladies cloakroom, and the mens is over there.

5   Theres a storm coming; wed better take shelter.

6   "It wasnt Aichas fault!" I shouted. "She couldnt help it."

7   Have you met the Smiths? Theyre from York.

8   Lets pop down to the newsagents.

9   My parents house was sold for a hundred thousand pounds.

10   Thats not my sons coat! Wheres James jacket?

Score: /10

II   Write the correct alternative in each blank.

A   Whose / Who's

1   _____ been using my pen?

2   _____ shoes are these?

3 _____ side are you on?

4 _____ that man over there?

B its / it's

    1 A leopard never changes _____ spots.

    2 _____ very warm in here.

    3 _____ no use crying over spilt milk.

    4 The owl kills _____ prey with _____ claws.

C theirs / there's

    1 _____ a hole in your sock.

    2 Why are they using our machine? What's wrong with _____?

    3 Is that ours or _____?

    4 _____ nothing we can do about it.

Score: /12

III Replace each underlined word with a single possessive pronoun.

e.g. It is my pen = It is mine.

1 My pen is not working. Can I borrow your pen?

2 His bedroom is larger than her bedroom.

3 Her bedroom is tidier than his bedroom.

4 Our garden is smaller than their garden.

5 Their garden is prettier than our garden.

Score: /5

(Answers: page 197)

as and *like*

Fill in each gap with *as*, *as if* or *like*.

1 He treats me _____ an idiot.

2 It looks _____ we are going to be late again!

3 Nobody understands me _____ my mother does.

4 His career _____ a professional footballer is over.

5 He works _____ a dog.

6 He works _____ a waiter.

7 A frog starts life _____ a tadpole.

8 They say she drinks _____ a fish.

9 She got the job, _____ I thought she would.

10 He looked at me _____ I were mad.

11 She behaved _____ nothing had happened.

12 _____ you can see, my hands are empty.

13 She looked _____ she had just seen a ghost.

14 He was treated _____ a king when he won the lottery.

Score: /14
(Answers: page 197)

Capital letters

In the following sentences, underline and correct those words which should start with a capital letter.

1 for many years it was thought that the nile was the longest river in the world. in 1969 however, it was finally decided that the mighty amazon in south america was 4,195 miles long, fifty more than the nile.

2 when sir walter raleigh introduced tabacco into england in the early 1600's, king james I wrote a booklet arguing against its use.

3 "have you met professor oshima? he's a very famous professor from tokyo."

4 my eldest brother is studying economics at essex university. when i leave school, i'm going to be a hairdresser.

5 my brother, tony, is a doctor. he lives in wales and he speaks welsh fluently. we usually see him at christmas and sometimes at easter.

Score: /5
(Answers: page 198)

Colons (:)

Place a colon, where appropriate, in the sentences below.

1 The whole area was dark and deserted no street lights, no house lights, nothing.

2 She had been smoking marijuana and taking other drugs since she was thirteen. Now, said Mrs Turner, she had gone on to something worse heroin.

3 When I got to the top, I saw a most spectacular sight five dragons were fighting five unicorns.

4 The notice said 'Private. Keep out!'

5 Samir can't come with us he's not old enough.

6 There was still one problem how were we going to get back in time?

7 And then I had a happy thought there was no school tomorrow.

8 One person, the American inventor Thomas Midgley (1889-1944), created what are considered to be two of today's biggest environmental evils chlorofluorocarbons (CFCs) and leaded petrol.

Score: /8

(Answers: page 198)

Commas 1: when to pause

Insert commas where appropriate in the sentences below.

1 The moon has no atmosphere and no water so no life is possible.

2 If air is blown into water bubbles rise to the surface.

3 People have been mining gold silver tin iron copper and lead for thousands of years.

4 Scientists have discovered that bees mosquitoes wasps and other stinging insects prefer to sting girls rather than boys.

5 The giraffe is the tallest of all living animals but scientists are unable to explain how it got its long neck.

6 One of the things that birds snakes frogs cows and humans all have in common is a backbone.

7 Even after their heads have been cut off some insects may live for as long as a year. They react automatically to light temperature humidity and other stimuli.

8   Although I have been to France several times I do not speak French.

9   According to legend a mermaid is a young girl who lives in the sea. Instead of legs she has the tail of a fish.

10 With the exception of the organ the piano is the most complex musical instrument.

11 With the possible exception of the cobra crocodiles kill more people than any other animal.

12 She opened the parcel saw what was inside and let out a shrill scream.

13 According to Yoko Fusako intends to sell her cottage and move back to the city.

14 We yawn when we are tired sleepy or bored.

Score: /14

(Answers: page 198)

Commas 2: how to pause

Insert commas where appropriate in the sentences below. Tick any sentence that does not require commas.

1   Among the most important peoples of ancient America were the Aztecs who lived in the valley in which Mexico City is situated.

2   I'd like you to meet the man who saved my life.

3   The Vatican City which is the official home of the Pope is the world's smallest country.

4   Penicillin which was discovered by Alexander Fleming has saved millions of lives.

5   Silver which is a precious metal is lighter than gold.

6   The human body has 636 muscles each with its own name.

7   The St Gotthard tunnel which runs beneath the Swiss Alps is the world's longest road tunnel.

8   The exam that we took this morning was dead easy.

9   A machine that washes dishes is called a dishwasher.

10 He wanted to give all his money to charity which seemed very reasonable to me.

11 I gave her the watch that I had found in the street.

12 The woman you were talking to is a very famous actress.

13 The 'Mona Lisa' which was painted by Leonardo da Vinci is the most easily recognised painting in the world.

14 My father who used to be a businessman is training to be a bus driver.

Score: /14
(Answers: page 199)

Commas 3: the comma and relative clauses

Supply commas where necessary in the sentences below. Tick any sentence that does not require commas.

1 The Austrialian Aborigines were the earliest-known inhabitants of Australia. The term *aborigine* which comes from the Latin words *ab origine* means 'from the beginning'.

2 Australia is one of the world's leading exporters of sugarcane which grows along the north-eastern coast.

3 The Arctic is dominated by the Arctic Ocean and a vast treeless plain called the tundra. Unlike Antarctica which is an ice-covered continent much of the Arctic consists of ice-covered seas.

4 Lake Baikal which is located in Siberia is the only lake in the world that is deep enough to have deep-sea fish.

5 Chess is a game that requires a great deal of concentration.

6 Unlike chess and draughts which are very ancient games the game of dominoes is comparatively new.

Score: /6
(Answers: page 199)

Common spelling errors

I Read the joke below. How many spelling mistakes (involving silent letters) can you find? Underline the mistakes. Then correct them.

"Has Simon got long to live?" Robert asked the nurse.

"I don't no," she replied. "Shall I fech the doctor?"

"Please," insisted Robert in a solem voice.

The doctor arrived some minutes later.

"Sorry to have kept you waiting, but I was stiching up one of my patients," he explained.

Robert came strait to the point: "How bad is it? How long has Simon got to live?"

"Not long, I'm afraid. He could die at any moment," the doctor ansered. "He's barely consious."

On hearing the bad news, Robert went immediately to see Simon, his frend and busness partner.

Simon was lying in bed, and he was so weak that he coud hardly speak. When he saw Robert sitting beside him, he raised his head from the pillow and began to wisper: "Robert ... Robert ..."

"Rest, Simon, rest," Robert advised, noting how gastly white Simon's skin had turned.

"Save your strenth."

"No," insisted the dying man. "I can't. I must clear my consience before I die."

"What's troubling you, Simon?" asked Robert, scraching his head.

"I have been a very bad partner, Robert. I have been disloyal to you. Do you know how I aquired my Mercedes? Well, I stole £50,000 from the office safe. And do you remember when you were taken to court for not having paid any tax for ten years? You were aquitted on a technicality, if you remember. Well, I was the one who reported you to the tax inspector. I was the one who told your wife about you and the blonde secretry. I was the one who...."

"Don't worry, Simon," replied Robert, neeling down beside him.

"Please, don't worry. I was the one who put poison in your cup of tea."

Score: /19

II Correct the spelling of each of the words below:

librey; luggige; necesary; ocasionally; oportunity; parralel; profesional; reccommend; sucesful; sissors; suprised; forign; colision; perticularly; acident

Score: /15
(Answers: page 200)

Comparisons

Write out the correct comparative / superlative form of each word in brackets.

1   Derek is definitely the (lazy) boy in the class!

2   I do a lot of exercise. That's why I am (healthy) and (fit) than you are.

3   She asked the children to play (quiet) as they were making too much noise.

4   Of the four brothers, Naseer is certainly the (good)-looking, but by no means is he the (clever).

5   This new machine works (efficient) than the old one.

6   You are too slow. You are the (slow) in the class. You need to learn to work (quick).

7   He arrived (early) than the others.

Score: /10
(Answers: page 200)

Concord

Underline the correct alternative in brackets.

1   Either Sharon or Tracey (is / are) lying.

2   There (is / are) hundreds of people outside!

3   Fortunately, neither of the drivers (was / were) injured.

4   Apparently, neither Craig nor Ian (wants / want) to help.

5   Each of these instruments (costs / cost) over £1,000.

6   Everybody (was / were) surprised at her attitude.

7   A number of books (is / are) missing from the library.

8   The number of people who (has / have) died in road accidents (has / have) doubled in the past year.

9   All the furniture in this room (is / are) antique.

10   Every animal and plant (eats / eat), or (is / are) eaten by, other things.

11   There (is / are) plenty of activities for the young in this centre.

12   Physics (is / are) my worst subject at school.

13   The team (is / are) training twice as hard this week because they are playing the league champions on Saturday.

14   There (is / are) a kitchen, a dining-room and a toilet downstairs.

Score: /16

(Answers: page 200)

Dashes (–)

I   Insert dashes where appropriate in the sentences below.

1   Even at that early hour it was not yet six o'clock he was immaculately dressed.

2   Everything that we know about dinosaurs and everything that we will ever know comes from fossils.

3   An unusual thing about the spotted hyena is that unlike most animals the female is larger than the male.

4   How could you speak to him your own father in such a way?

5   Even my brother who is not known for his sense of humour had to laugh when I told him what had happened.

Score: /5

II   Insert dashes where appropriate in the sentences below:

1   The longest jump that has ever been recorded was a great bound of forty-two feet made by a kangaroo back in 1951 though, of course, it cannot be proved that there have not been even longer unrecorded ones.

2   He was a tall, lean man with thinning hair and a pleasant face the kind of face one would find hard to remember.

3   He smiled again a cold, hard smile.

4   An iceberg larger than Belgium was observed in the South Pacific in 1956. It was 208 miles long and 60 miles wide the largest ever seen.

5   The longest underwater cable is nine thousand miles long, and it runs all the way from Australia to Port Alberni, Canada. It is known as COMPAC the Commonwealth Pacific Cable.

Score: /5

(Answers: page 200)

Direct speech

Correct the passage below. Use capital letters, speech marks and other punctuation marks where appropriate.

> he looked at her and said where did you get that from
> i found it she said it was on the floor
> i don't believe you he shouted at the top of his voice
> there's no need to shout she said in a firm voice
> give it to me he growled or you'll be sorry

Score: /5

(Answers: page 201)

Emphatic English

Finish each sentence in such a way that it means exactly the same as the sentence above it.

1   He lost everything because of his greed.

    It was ⎯⎯⎯⎯⎯⎯⎯⎯⎯⎯⎯⎯⎯⎯ .

2   You will not find such generous and spontaneous hospitality anywhere else in the world.

    Nowhere ⎯⎯⎯⎯⎯⎯⎯⎯⎯⎯⎯⎯⎯ .

3   The news was so shocking that nobody knew what to say.

    So ⎯⎯⎯⎯⎯⎯⎯⎯⎯⎯⎯⎯⎯⎯⎯ .

4   We never suspected that the money had been stolen.

    At no ⎯⎯⎯⎯⎯⎯⎯⎯⎯⎯⎯⎯⎯⎯ .

5   They didn't tell me about it until later.

    Only ⎯⎯⎯⎯⎯⎯⎯⎯⎯⎯⎯⎯⎯⎯ .

6   It may seem strange, but he quite likes being in prison.

    Strange ⎯⎯⎯⎯⎯⎯⎯⎯⎯⎯⎯⎯⎯ .

7   Even though I admire her courage, I think it is foolish of her to go there on her own.

    Much ⎯⎯⎯⎯⎯⎯⎯⎯⎯⎯⎯⎯⎯⎯ .

8   He may be good at languages, but he is hopeless at Maths.

Good _____ .

Score: /8
(Answers: page 201)

Formal English

Where possible, change *who* to *whom* in the sentences below. Tick any sentence where it is not possible to do so.

1   She was introduced to a man called Smith, who she vaguely recognised.

2   'The world tolerates conceit from those who are successful, but not from anybody else.' (John Blake)

3   'Almost all absurdity of conduct arises from the imitation of those who we cannot resemble.' (Samuel Johnson)

Score: /3
(Answers: page 201)

Greek and Latin roots

I   A number of English words are derived from *dictus*, the past participle of the Latin verb *dicere* (= to say). How many English words can you think of that either begin or end with the root element *dict*?

Score: one mark per word

II   Choosing from the words given, add a suitable prefix or suffix to each uncompleted word below:

anti (= against), *arch* (= main / chief)
fore (= before / a head), *hyper* (= too / extremely)
phobia (= fear / hatred), *pseudo* (= false / pretending to be)
retro (= backward / backwards)

1   Everybody in the team felt despondent when they were beaten 2–0 by their _____ -*rivals*.

2   You're just talking _____ -*intellectual* nonsense!

3   This material is _____ *sensitive* to light.

4   *Claustro* _____ is the fear of enclosed places.

5   In _____ *spect*, it is easy to see where we went wrong.

6   She claims she can _____ *tell* the future.

7   He was arrested during the _____ -*war* demonstration.

8   Food additives can make children _____ *active*.

9   Not wishing to use her real name, she wrote the novel under a _____ *nym*.

10 Their victory was a _____ *gone* conclusion.

Score: /10

(Answers: page 201)

Homophones

I   Underline and correct any spelling mistakes in the sentences below.

1   I was very surprised when she walked straight passed me without even saying 'hello'.

2   I wasn't sure weather he was joking or not when he said he was going to wring my neck.

3   The frail old man looked quite pail.

4   Behind a fur tree lurked a bear waiting for its prey.

5   He intends to buy some new softwear for his computer.

6   We had to dress very formerly for the occasion.

7   It pored with rain and we all got soaked.

8   We were extremely greatful to them for their support.

Score: /8

II Underline the correct alternative in brackets.

1   She is (to / too / two) clever by half!

2   I am tired. Let's have a (break / brake).

3   The (reign / rein / rain) in Spain falls mainly on the (plane / plain).

4   You can buy (stationery / stationary) at that shop.

5   He asked me (which / witch) one I preferred.

6   Spiders (pray / prey) on small flies.

7   (Who's / Whose) book is this?

8   She was forced to (flea / flee).

9   He was the (soul / sole) survivor.

10   We need to (alter / altar) the schedule.

11   Aeroplanes are kept in (hangars / hangers).

12   He was admitted to hospital for some (minor / miner) surgery.

13   The soldiers were asked to shoot on (site / sight).

14   The author asked the distinguished professor to (right / write / rite) a (foreword / forward) to his new book.

15   He tried to (prise / prize) open the box with a knife.

16   Would you like some breakfast (serial / cereal)?

17   That particular popstar was her (idle / idol).

18   He has a (sore / soar) throat.

Score: /20
(Answers: page 201)

Hyphens (-)

Supply hyphens where appropriate in the sentences below.

1   Mr Hook is an ill tempered, pig headed, hard hearted secondary school teacher.

2   She was wearing a white hat and a silver coloured dress.

3   He was a grey bearded, middle aged man with a reddish face.

4   With Peter was a rather thick set, pleasant looking man in his mid thirties.

5   He was a tall one eyed man with a serious looking face.

6   She gave me some home baked cake and a glass of fresh orange juice.

7   Cyrano de Bergerac, seventeenth century poet, wit and expert swordsman, fought and won at least one thousand duels over insults about his extra large nose. During one three month period, he 'ran through' four people each week.

8   Anna's husband to be is a hard headed businessman who owns a multi storey car park near the town centre.

9   "I am fed up with being treated like a ten year old child!" complained Bouchra. "I am actually eleven years old!"

10 Father to son: "I know there's a big crack in the sitting room wall, but that's no reason to go telling everyone that you come from a broken home."

Score: /10
(Answers: page 202)

Irregular verbs

The following verbs in brackets need to be in the past tense. Change the form of the verb where necessary. Tick any verb that does not need to change.

1   We (catch) the first available train, but then (find) we had (get) on the wrong train.

2   I got (sting) by a bee and it really (hurt).

3   At half-time the score was 4-nil, and we (think) we had (lose) the match. But in the second half we (fight) back really hard and (win) the game by five goals to four.

4   My little brother (spread) the butter all over his face and we all (burst) out laughing.

5   We (hold) hands as we (slide) down the muddy hill.

6   They (keep) on teasing me.

7   When he (bend) down, he (split) his trousers.

8   I was (teach) to swim by my father.

9   She (stick) her tongue out at me, and that (make) me really mad.

10 We (spend) the whole day on the beach and (build) a huge sandcastle that (can) be seen for miles around.

Score: /10
(Answers: page 202)

Loose English

I Finish each sentence in such a way that it means exactly the same as the sentence above it.

1 Her eyesight is better than mine.

   a She has _____ .

   b She can _____ .

2 The model aeroplane costs £10, whereas the model car costs £40.

   The model car is four _____ .

3 We are thinking of moving because we are not satisfied with any of the schools in our area.

   The reason _____ .

4 Do you mind if we postpone the meeting until tomorrow?

   Would it be all right if _____ .

Score: /5

II In which of the following sentences is there a mistake? Tick any sentence that is grammatically correct.

1 He's been sat there since eight o' clock this morning.

2 We sat at the back of the cinema.

3 She was sat in an armchair, knitting a jumper.

4 She sat next to me on the coach.

Score: /4

(Answers: page 202)

Negative prefixes

Underline the correct alternative in italics.

1 She did not want to *dissapoint / disappoint* her parents.

2 This report is *unnofficial / unofficial*.

3 He slipped into the house *unnoticed / unoticed*.

4 She *dissagreed / disagreed* with what we said.

5 Why did the soldiers *dissobey / disobey* the order?

161

6 *Iregular / Irregular* verbs should be learnt by heart.

7 They discovered that he was *iliterate / illiterate*.

8 It is *inadvisable / innadvisable* to take a bath straight after a meal.

9 He said the charity's funds were being *missused / misused*.

10 He was accused of being *dissloyal / disloyal*.

Score: /10

(Answers: page 202)

Nouns 1

I Complete each word with one of the following suffixes: *-er, -or, -ar*.

1 a translat___	2 a smuggl___	3 gramm___
4 a trait___	5 a solicit___	6 a lawy___
7 a radiat___	8 an announc___	9 a spectat___
10 a caterpill___	11 a li___	12 a doct___
13 a sail___	14 a coll___	15 a dictat___
16 a prison___	17 a visit___	18 a word-process___
19 an auth___	20 a burgl___	

Score: /20

II Complete each word with one of the following suffixes: *-er, -or, -ar*.

1 a surviv___	2 a begg___	3 an inspect___
4 vineg___	5 an edit___	6 a garden___
7 a govern___	8 a ventilat___	9 a comput___
10 a thermomet___		

Score: /10

III Where a word is incomplete, insert either *-ence* or *-ance*.

1 Abs_____ makes the heart grow fonder.

2 'If a man does not make new acquaint_____s as he advances through life, he will soon find himself alone.' (Samuel Johnson)

3 'But with the morning, cool repent_____ came.' (Sir Walter Scott)

4 'Had we lived, I should have had a tale to tell of the hardihood, endur_____ and courage of my companions which would have stirred the heart of every Englishman. These rough notes and our dead bodies must tell the tale.' (Robert Falcon Scott)

5 'Beware that you do not lose the subst_____ by grasping at the shadow.' (Aesop)

6 'Sil_____ is the virtue of fools.' (Francis Bacon)

7 'A sufficient and sure method of civilisation is the influ_____ of good women.' (Emerson)

8 'It is ridiculous for any man to criticise the works of another if he has not distinguished himself by his own perform_____s.' (Addison)

9 'Knowledge is the child of experi_____ .' (Leonardo da Vinci)

10 'The differ_____ between journalism and literature is that journalism is unreadable and literature is never read.' (Oscar Wilde)

11 Leonard Bacon, a famous nineteenth-century American theologian, was once addressing a religious confer_____ when he said something that annoyed a member of the audi_____ . "Why, I never heard of such a thing in all my life!" shouted the outraged man. "I'm terribly sorry," said Bacon, "but I cannot allow your ignor_____ , however vast, to prejudice my knowledge, however small."

Score: /13
(Answers: page 202)

Nouns 2

To complete each sentence below, form a noun ending in -*ness* or -*ment* from the word in brackets.

1 He assured her that her (happy) was his prime concern.

2 We were impressed by the (friendly) of the hotel staff.

3 He was proud of his (achieve).

4 He gave a lecture on the (ugly) of modern architecture.

5 In his (excite), he forgot to leave his name and address.

6 When taking this medicine, some people may experience the following side-effects: (dizzy) and (dry) in the mouth.

Score: /7
(Answers: page 203)

Passive voice

Make the following statements more formal by changing them from active to passive.

1 Sometimes you can see shining coloured lights, called aurorae, in the skies above the North and South Poles.

2 People have kept wild animals in zoos since ancient times.

3 A lot of people consider ice hockey to be the fastest game in the world.

4 People say that Mark Twain wrote most of his books in bed.

5 They have postponed the election until next month.

6 We call the study of fossils paleontology.

7 In India they regard the cow as a sacred animal.

8 You are not allowed to smoke in this area.

9 We find owls of one species or another in all parts of the world.

10 In ancient times, people thought that the owl was an unlucky bird.

Score: /10
(Answers: page 203)

Plain English

Just for fun, rephrase the following in plain English. Don't worry if you can't make head or tail of any of the sentences; it's not your fault.

1 How would you assess the dynamics of his interaction with his colleagues?

2 He shows little personal capacity for radical innovation.

3 Our company has at its core the mission of being one of the most flexible, cost-effective and high-quality suppliers of bureau services available. We are currently looking to employ proactive individuals to assist us in meeting this mission.

4 He is equipped with effective people management skills.

5 My father is a domestic refurbishment consultant.

6 My brother is vertically challenged for his age.

7 I am afraid that, with regard to Mr Wilkins, we have a negative patient outcome.

164

8   The missile attack caused some collateral damage.

Score: /8
(Answers: page 203)

Plurals

Change each underlined noun from singular to plural.

1   The bear was attacked by a pack of <u>wolf</u>.

2   No adult has ever actually proved that <u>elf</u>, <u>goblin</u> and <u>fairy</u> do not exist.

3   For over 1,500 years there have been <u>story</u> about a mysterious creature living at the bottom of Loch Ness in Scotland.

4   Many years ago people believed that black cats were <u>witch</u> in disguise.

5   Nearly all the large <u>city</u> in the world were once small <u>village</u>.

6   <u>Octopus</u> are not as dangerous as they look or are made out to be, but they can be unpleasant.

7   King Henry VIII had six <u>wife</u>.

8   He ate four <u>sandwich</u>, two <u>bunch</u> of <u>banana</u>, ten <u>sausage</u> and a packet of <u>biscuit</u>. He didn't have an ice cream because he said he was on a diet.

Score: /15
(Answers: page 204)

Prepositions

Underline the correct alternative in brackets.

1   It took years of research, but (at / in) the end they found a cure for the disease.

2   He was eventually cured (from / of) the disease and was able to lead a normal life.

3   Everybody applauded (at / in) the end of the performance.

4   The audience was (comprised / composed / consisted) mainly of teenagers.

5   For him, happiness consists (of / in) having no responsibilities.

6   Cheese is made (of / from) milk.

7   I am not sure what this statue is made (of / from). Marble, I think.

8   Whilst the others slept, he set out in search (for / of) firewood and water.

9   There has been some improvement (in / on) his work.

10   This offer is certainly a vast improvement (in / on) their previous one.

11   (In / On) principle I agree (with / to) what you are saying, but we have to be realistic.

12   We managed to persuade him to agree (with / to) our request.

13   To be honest, I am surprised (at / by) her.

14   In the exam, the students were asked to compare the economy of post-war Japan (with / to) that of Italy.

15   Only you and (I / me) need know about this.

16   They want to come on holiday with my sister and (I / me).

17   My taste in music differs (from / to) hers.

18   It was different (to / than) what I had expected.

19   She said that she was fed up (with / of) her present job.

Score: /20
(Answers: page 204)

Regular verbs in the past

Change each verb in brackets so that it ends in -ed.

He (stare) at the old lady just ahead of him in the queue. He was certain he (recognise) her. Wasn't she the actress who had (star) in 'Silver Moon' some fifty years ago? He had (enjoy) the film very much and, like so many boys of his generation, had (worship) the beautiful star as a goddess.

He vaguely (recall) that she had (quarrel) with an important film producer who had, subsequently, (cancel) her contract and, effectively, (ruin) her career.

He (wonder) whether he should say something to her. Perhaps she (prefer) not to be (remind) of the dim and distant past, of dreams that had never been (fulfil).

As he (hesitate), a taxi (pull) up. Almost bent double and with the aid of a walking stick, she (shuffle) forward. He (open) his mouth and ...

Score: /17
(Answers: page 204)

Relative pronouns

Complete the sentences below with *who*, *whom*, *whose* or *which*.

1   Jogging is an activity _____ is good for your health.

2   In the United Kingdom there is only one poisonous snake, the adder, _____ is found in most parts.

3   Mushrooms are fungi. Fungi are plants _____ do not have green leaves or flowers.

4   Do you know anybody _____ can help me with this problem?

5   There was once a farmer _____ name was Bill.

6   I'd like to know _____ gave you that information.

7   With _____ am I speaking?

8   Thirteen is a number _____ many people consider to be unlucky.

9   Look! That's the woman _____ purse was stolen.

10 From _____ did you obtain that information?

Score: /10
(Answers: page 204)

Starting and finishing a sentence

I   Divide the words below into four sentences.

snakes are cold-blooded creatures they are only as hot or cold as the air around them that is why you don't find many snakes in cool countries such as Britain it's simply too chilly for them to stay alive.

Score: /4

II Correct the sentences below. Each sentence should begin with a capital letter and finish either with a question mark (?) or an exclamation mark (!).

1   what is her name

2   what a surprise

3   how embarrassing

4   how did it happen

5   do you know the answer

6   do it now

Score: /6

(Answers: page 204)

Suffixes

❙   **1**   Add *-ed* to the words below and make any other necessary changes.

spot ___	row ___	pop ___
ban ___	cry ___	hum ___
tape ___	play ___	peer ___
tap ___	slap ___	peep ___

2   Add *-ing* to the words below and make any other necessary changes.

dig ___	heat ___	run ___
slim ___	hit ___	sew ___
sweat ___	fly ___	stare ___
gaze ___	shine ___	star ___

3   Add *-er* to the words below and make any other necessary changes.

great ___	cool ___	mug ___
big ___	mix ___	rob ___
thin ___	wet ___	print ___
fat ___	wait ___	

4   Add *-est* to the words below and make any other necessary changes.

fast ___	late ___	dry ___
sad ___	nice ___	hot ___
large ___		

5   Add *-en* to the words below and make any other necessary changes.

deaf ___	wool ___	soft ___
rot ___	wood ___	glad ___
sad ___	mad ___	

6   Add *-ish* to the words below and make any other necessary changes.

red ____   blue ____   child ____

snob ____   fool ____

Score: /55

II   1   Add *-ed* to the words below and make any other necessary changes.

commit ____   offer ____   appeal ____

refer ____   cancel ____   panic ____

2   Add *-ing* to the words below and make any other necessary changes.

prefer ____   conceal ____   benefit ____

quarrel ____   develop ____   begin ____

3   Add *-ence* to the words below and make any other necessary changes.

occur ____   prefer ____   differ ____

refer ____   excel ____

4   Add *-ation* to the words below and make any other necessary changes.

instal ____   imagine ____   transport ____

cancel ____   limit ____

Score: /22

(Answers: page 204)

Unnecessary words

Cross out any unnecessary words in the sentences below.

1   She looked utterly and completely exhausted.

2   I am dreadfully and truly sorry about what happened the other day.

3   She asked her students to work in pairs of twos.

4   The student was told to rewrite the essay again.

5   The sheets were still slightly wet and damp.

6   There are two different kinds of speech: formal and informal speech.

7   He was asked whether he had ever taken illegal drugs at any time.

8   During the course of the race, two of the horses slipped and fell.

9   Personally I think that he has made the right decision.

10   When we got to the hotel, the manager was there in person to greet us.

11   Within a few weeks of being released from prison, he had reverted back to his old ways.

12   Therefore for that reason, I feel I have no option but to resign.

13   The coach departs at 6 a.m. in the morning.

14   He made so many mistakes and errors that the teacher told him to repeat the exercise again.

15   "What an unexpected surprise!" she exclaimed.

16   If you refer back to your notes, you will see that we have already covered that topic.

17   I rushed quickly down the stairs and opened the front door.

18   The car broke down and we had to walk the rest of the way on foot.

19   We asked him to keep the report as short and brief as possible.

20   The concert was so boring that the children yawned and fidgeted throughout the whole performance.

Score: /20
(Answers: page 205)

Tricky verbs

Underline the correct alternative in brackets.

1   He said that he was just going to (lay / lie) down for a while.

2   Do you think you'll be able to (lay / lie) the carpet today?

3   He (lay / laid) a firm hand on my shoulder.

4   They found him (laying / lying) on the floor.

5   To cover their costs, they had to (raise / rise) their prices.

6   The price of popular toys always (raises / rises) just before Christmas.

7   My mum's been (learning / teaching) me to swim.

8   He was (hung / hanged) for murder.

9   I phoned to apologise but she just (hung / hanged) up on me.

10 We (was / were) pleased with the result.

11 They (was / were) surprised to find that I (was / were) from the same village.

12 "If I (was / were) you, I'd give up smoking," said the doctor.

13 "It (doesn't / don't) work," she complained.

14 "If she (doesn't / don't) turn up soon, we'll have to go without her," he said.

Score: /15

(Answers: page 205)

Word endings 1

Complete each word with either -ible or -able.

respons _____ ; sens _____ ; advis _____ ;

avail _____ ; incred _____ ; irrit _____ ;

flex _____ ; poss _____ ; reli _____ ;

vis _____

Score: /10

(Answers: page 205)

Word endings 2

Where a word is incomplete, complete it with either -ent or -ant.

1 He made himself a cup of inst_____ coffee.

2 He looks really eleg_____ in his new suit.

3 The strong curr_____ carried the boat downstream.

4 She is a persist_____ tru_____ .

5 We spent a pleas_____ day in the countryside.

6 She was reluct_____ to admit that she was wrong.

7 The police are investigating the incid_____ .

8 The view from the top was magnific_____ .

9 I am looking for a perman _____ job.

10 The matter is extremely urg_____ .

11 Your work is excell_____ .

12 You think he's brilli_____ ; I think he's ignor_____ !

13 Is this a conveni_____ moment?

14 The hospital holds special classes for expect_____ mothers.

15 He knows some of the most emin_____ scientists in Europe.

16 He thanked her for the pres_____ .

17 That was very observ_____ of you.

18 There was one applic_____ for the vac_____ post.

19 He was told not to be so insol_____ .

20 The judge decided to be leni_____ .

21 She asked if they had any blackcurr_____ jam.

22 We are almost totally reli_____ on imported oil.

Score: /25
(Answers: page 205)

Word endings 3

Where a word is incomplete, add one of the following endings: -*ary*, -*ery*, -*ory*, -*ury*.

1 Every student should have a diction_____ .

2 Where is the nearest libr_____ ?

3 He is here in an advis_____ capacity only.

4 The general word for sweets of all kinds is 'confection_____' .

5 He has fond memories of his prim_____ school.

6 His birthday is in Febru_____ .

7 Is he looking for a tempor_____ or a permanent position?

8 It is compuls_____ to study English at school.

9 The students had to write a summ_____ of what they had read.

10 An itiner_____ is a detailed plan of a journey.

11 He was sent to prison for committing perj_____ .

12 She is suffering from loss of mem_____ .

13 What an extraordin_____ thing to say!

14 He predicted a landslide vict_____ for the Conservatives.

15 Tomorrow is their wedding annivers _____ .

16 She used to work as a secret_____ .

17 He leads a solit_____ existence.

18 The lion is a predat_____ beast.

19 The scen_____ in Switzerland is magnificent.

20 In some countries you can be imprisoned for adult_____ .

21 A tribut_____ is a river or stream which discharges its waters into a larger river or stream.

22 An estu_____ is the broad mouth of a river when it widens out before reaching the sea.

23 I am not bored. On the contr_____ , I think this is fascinating.

24 He comes from Hung_____ .

25 Haemophilia is a heredit_____ disease.

26 An animal will always defend its territ_____ .

27 He asked if he could use the lavat_____ .

Score: /27

(Answers: page 206)

Word endings 4

Where a word is incomplete, add -*us*, -*ous*, -*ious* or -*eous*.

1 All the characters portrayed in this novel are fictit_____ .

2 Is that disease contag_____ ?

3 He appeared obliv_____ to his surroundings.

4 He said he had never eaten octop_____ before.

5 He was the victim of a particularly vic_____ attack.

6   Who's that suspic_____ -looking man?

7   What a hid_____ shirt!

8   How can you afford to rent such a luxur_____ flat?

9   He admitted that he had been wrong the prev_____ time.

10   The effect was instantan_____ .

11   He tried to impress us, but we found him rather pretent_____ .

12   She was a shy but conscient_____ student.

Score: /12
(Answers: page 206)

Words 1

Underline the correct alternative in brackets.

1   I was not (all together / altogether) surprised.

2   It doesn't matter which book. (Any one / Anyone) will do.

3   You can take (any one / anyone) of these cakes.

4   Did (any one / anyone) see what actually happened?

5   (Every one / Everyone) of these pictures is a fake.

6   There's (no one / noone) here. (Every one / Everyone) has gone.

7   She visits her grandmother (every day / everyday).

8   You are not going (all ready / already), are you?

9   If you are (all ready / already), we shall begin.

10   (May be / Maybe) I'll see her tonight.

11   I (may be / maybe) able to help her.

12   There (may be / maybe) trouble ahead.

13   Is there (any way / anyway) we can help?

14   I just wanted to (thank you / thankyou) for all your help.

15   She sat (in front / infront) of us.

16 Take a jacket (in case / incase) it gets cold.

17 I am sorry, but I (can not / cannot) stand her!

18 He has gone to the local (super market / supermarket).

19 "This is Sue, my (flat mate / flatmate)."

Score: /20

(Answers: page 206)

Words 2

How many spelling mistakes can you find in the sentences below? Underline and correct each mistake.

1 Jericho, in Jordan, is the oldest town in the world. People have lived there for allmost ten thousand years.

2 I have allready told her that she is not welcome here.

3 The sun's harmfull ultra-violet rays are filtered out by the ozone layer.

4 Going for a walk in the park is a traditional family passtime.

5 We had informed him that he must fulfill his obligations.

6 It was a delight to watch such a skillful and gracefull dancer.

7 I am not alltogether happy with their decisions.

8 Her granson can be a bit of a handfull at times.

9 You are not allowed to wear earings at school.

10 Two old ladies were saying farewel to their beloved vicar who was moving on to another parish.

"We shall miss you ever so much, vicar," said the first lady in a sorrowfull voice. "And we shall especially miss your sermons."

"Oh yes, we shall indeed," agreed the second tearfuly. "We never knew what sin really was untill you came here."

Score: /15

(Answers: page 206)

Appendix 1

Confusing words 1

Look carefully at the sentences below. Tick those sentences that are correct. Underline and correct any word that has been misused.

1   He's still suffering from the effects of the drugs he took.

2   The film had quite an affect on her.

3   The noise outside is effecting my concentration.

4   My grandmother is not averse to the odd gin and tonic.

5   The company has had a lot of averse publicity recently.

6   He is under the allusion that he is next in line for promotion.

7   It made a change to have such an appreciable audience.

8   There has been an appreciative drop in the number of students attending his class.

9   The workbook and cassette compliment the course book.

10 The President of the United States and his press corpse arrived early this morning.

11 The mountain was enveloped in mist.

12 They were warned that a strike was eminent.

13 The teacher found it difficult to illicit a coherent response from the student.

14 I recognise him, but his name alludes me.

15 During her speech, she alluded to the lack of co-operation she had received from certain members of staff.

16 Can you wait? I will make some enquiries.

17 Although he doesn't say so openly, his distrust of modern technology is explicit in everything he writes.

18 One cannot change humane nature.

19 Many people regard fox-hunting as inhuman.

20 It was rather ingenious of her to ask a complete stranger to look after her luggage while she went to buy a ticket.

Score: /20
(Answers: page 207)

Confusing words 2

Correct any errors in the sentences below. Tick any sentence that is correct.

1 He implied from her comments that all was not well.

2 The unexpected victory boosted the team's morals.

3 In the 200 metres and the 400 metres, Fergus came first and third respectfully.

4 She shrugged her shoulders and gave a regrettable smile.

5 The boat was especially constructed to withstand arctic conditions.

6 It is easier to hit a stationery target.

7 He said that he was disinterested in politics.

8 He won't do it. He says it's against his principals.

9 You'll have to pay for any excess luggage.

10 She's loathe to admit that she is in the wrong.

11 It sounds fine in principal, but will it work in practice?

12 Does this store have a stationary department?

13 It is your morale duty to help her.

14 What are you inferring? Are you calling me a liar?

15 Becky, Gillian and Hazel were dressed in pink, blue and yellow respectively.

16 Package holidays, specially to Spain and Greece, are much cheaper than they were last year.

17 We stock plastic chairs and wooden ones, but the later are rather expensive.

Score: /17
(Answers: page 207)

Confusing words 3

Underline the correct alternative in brackets.

1 The air strike (afflicted / inflicted) heavy casualties on the enemy troops.

2 I need (some time / sometime) to think about it. I will give you my answer (some time / sometime) next week.

3   She spent half an hour (filing / filling) her nails.

4   A (flare / flair) is often used as a distress signal at sea.

5   "I've (forgotten / left) the tickets," he murmured as they entered the theatre. "I've (forgotten / left) them in the hotel room."

6   She was wearing a very pretty (broach / brooch).

7   The trouble with him is that he likes to (flaut / flout) his wealth.

8   All her teachers say that she has a (flair / flare) for Maths.

9   They (baited / bated) the trap with a live goat and waited for the tiger to appear.

10   Charlie Watkins, (some time / sometime) soldier of fortune and ex-security guard, was found murdered in his flat last night.

11   I wish he would keep his views to himself and not (afflict / inflict) them on us at every possible opportunity.

12   They stayed in a (luxurious / luxuriant) hotel.

13   What's the name of the actress who plays the (heroin / heroine) in the film?

14   In medieval times, bear-(baiting / bating) was a popular form of entertainment.

15   She is (afflicted / inflicted) with arthritis and can barely walk.

16   "If you continue to (flaunt / flout) the law," warned the judge, "I'll have no alternative but to send you to prison."

Score: /18

(Answers: page 207)

Confusing words 4

Underline the correct alternative in brackets.

1   He is a highly (emotional / emotive) person and has been known to burst into tears while making a speech.

2   Under an (authoritarian / authoritative) regime, people do not have the freedom to act as they wish.

3   His behaviour was so (contemptible / contemptuous) that everybody gave him the cold shoulder.

4   The surgeon explained that he would have to remove the (deceased / diseased) kidney.

5   People will not stop using their cars until we have a more (efficient / effective) public transport system.

6   He was a bit too smooth for my liking. I was not impressed by his (urban / urbane) charm and wit.

7   The inspector said that the machinery was (defective / deficient) and needed replacing.

8   As we were crossing the (desert / dessert), a sand storm caught us (unaware / unawares).

9   You should not light a match near (inflammable / non-flammable) material.

10 Professor Thomson's book – considered by many to be the (definite / definitive) work on the subject – gives an (authoritarian / authoritative) account of events leading up to the Spanish Civil War.

11 Legalised abortion is an (emotional / emotive) issue.

12 It was an (odious / odorous) crime and he deserves to be imprisoned for life.

13 He defended the film by claiming that it was (erotic / exotic) rather than pornographic.

14 He replied in such a (contemptible / contemptuous) tone that she took offence and stormed out of the office.

15 Friends and relatives of the (deceased / diseased) attended a special memorial service.

Score: /17
(Answers: page 207)

Appendix 2

Words ending in -*k*, -*ck* and -*ke*

There is one spelling mistake in each of the sentences below. Underline and correct the mistake.

1   You are jocking, aren't you ?

2   He was as thin as a rack.

3   The child was knoked down by a lorry.

4   We bought two cakes and a paket of biscuits.

5   We had chiken for lunch.

6   It was very cold, so I put on a jaket.

7   He showed us a few triks.

8   I was really shoked when she told us what had happened.

9   He kicked the ball too hard and brocke a window.

10 After breckfast, we went for a walk.

Score: /10

(Answers: page 208)

Appendix 3

Problems of usage

Underline the correct alternative in brackets.

1   Are you (quite / quiet) sure you know what you are doing?

2   Could you show me (where / were) you found the object?

3   What shall we have for (desert / dessert)?

4   Do you have a spare (envelop / envelope)?

5   The team will (consist / comprise) of the following: Mark, John,...

6   The house was struck by (lightening / lightning).

7   You should learn to be more (tolerable / tolerant) of others.

8   You are too (trusting / trustworthy). That's why people take advantage of you.

9   I am feeling rather (alone / lonely).

Score: /9

(Answers: page 208)

Answer key

Answer key

1 Adjectives 1

1 silly, these*, lovely
2 This*, terrible, sorry

2 Adjectives 2

1 boring
2 interested
3 amazing
4 satisfied
5 amusing
6 amused
7 annoyed
8 annoying
9 pleasing
10 worried

3 Adjectives 3

1 impossible
2 illegal
3 irregular
4 dishonest
5 unusual
6 unimportant
7 unnecessary
8 immature
9 impatient
10 invisible

4 Adjectives 4

1 cheapest, easiest
2 dirtiest

3 smaller, shorter
4 bigger
5 largest

5 Adverbs 1

I 1 beautifully
   2 carefully
   3 quietly, calmly
   4 heavily

II 1 slow = slowly
   2 real = really
   3 easy = easily
   4 gentle = gently

6 Adverbs 2

Unfortunately, regrettably, extremely, utterly, occasionally, truly, immediately, gladly, humbly, happily, incredibly, simply, easily, really, sincerely

7 Adverbs 3

1 correct
2 quickly
3 carefully, slowly
4 correct
5 quietly
6 well
7 strong = correct, easily
8 correct
9 correct
10 neatly

* 'these' and 'This' are demonstrative adjectives,

8 American and British spelling

1 neighbour's behaviour
2 favourite colour
3 licence
4 offence
5 programme
6 acceptable
7 enrol
8 acceptable

9 Apostrophes 1

Four apostrophes are needed:

We're having; The weather's been; it's beginning; you're enjoying

10 Apostrophes 2

I 1 yours
2 ours
3 Hers
4 theirs

II architect's
politician's
politician's
architect's
It's
politician's

11 *as* and *like*

1 as
2 like
3 like
4 as if
5 as if
6 like
7 as
8 as
9 as if
10 As

12 Capital letters

I An Englishman, a Scotsman and a Welshman were stranded on a small island in the Atlantic Ocean. One day they found a magic lamp. When they rubbed it, a genie appeared and granted each of them one wish.

"I'd like to be back in Birmingham," said the Englishman. Puff! He disappeared.

"I'd like to be back in Glasgow," said the Scotsman. Puff! He disappeared.

"Gosh," said the Welshman, "I'm very lonely here on my own. I wish my friends were back again."

Puff! Puff!

II My, Thomas Smythe, I, Sheffield, I, April, I, I've, Bono, I, French, I, Spanish, I've, Spain, My, English, 'Slick Girls', I, I, Sheffield United, My, England

13 Colons (:)

I The rainbow has seven colours: red, orange, yellow, green, blue, indigo and violet.

II 1 The dodo was a big flightless bird. There are no dodos left alive today: they are extinct.

2 There is not much difference between rabbits and hares: they both have long ears and long back legs. Hares are slightly larger and move by jumping, whereas rabbits move by running.

14 Commas 1

1 "Yes, but I can't go." "The invitation says 4 to 7, and I am eight."

2 "Dad, will you do my homework for me?" "No, it wouldn't be right." "Well, at least you can try."

3 Traveller: Excuse me, do you have a room for tonight? Hotel Proprietor: Certainly, sir. It'll be £50 a night, or I can let you have a room for only £10 if you make your own bed. Traveller: I'll take the £10 room. Hotel Proprietor: Right! I'll just go and fetch the wood, the hammer and the nails for the bed.

15 Commas 2

Note: Commas indicated in brackets (,) are optional.

1 As two men were walking along the seashore, they found an oyster and began to quarrel about it.

"I saw it first," said one of the men, "so it belongs to me."

"I picked it up," said the other, "so I have a right to keep it."

As they were quarrelling (,) a lawyer came by (,) and they asked him to decide for them in the matter.

The lawyer agreed to do so, but before he would give his opinion he required the two men to give him their assurance that they would agree to whatever he decided.

Then the lawyer said, "It seems to me that you both have a claim to the oyster; so I will divide it between you, and you will then be perfectly satisfied."

Opening the oyster, he quickly ate it and(,) very gravely(,) handed an empty shell to each of the men.

"But you have eaten the oyster!" cried the men.

"Ah, that was my fee for deciding the case!" said

the lawyer. "But I have divided all that remains in a perfectly fair and just manner."

That is what happens when two quarrelsome persons go to law about something that they cannot agree upon.

Note: Commas indicated in brackets (,) are optional.

2   When the steamship *Stella* left Southampton on the afternoon before Good Friday in the year 1899, she was bound for the Channel Islands(,) with nearly two hundred passengers on board.

Not long after the ship had started her voyage, the sea became covered with fog. The captain hoped it would lift, and kept the ship at full speed. But the fog grew thicker(,) and the *Stella* crashed on some rocks. The lifeboats were lowered(,) and the passengers behaved as bravely as men and women can in a crisis.

But the name of one woman will always be remembered when people think of the sinking of the *Stella*. Mrs Mary Rogers, the stewardess, comforted the women and gave each of them a life-belt, fastening it with her own hands. She led them to the side of the sinking ship, where the boats were being lowered. At the last moment(,) it was found that one woman had no life-belt. Instantly(,) the stewardess took off her own belt and gave it up and the woman was lifted safely into the boat. The sailors called to the stewardess to jump in but the boat was full.

"No, no!" she said. "There is no room. One more and the boat will sink."

The ship sank into the sea, and Mary Rogers looked on the world for the last time.

"Goodbye, goodbye!" she cried, and then: "Lord, take me!"

Within a minute (,) the *Stella* was gone, and with her the brave stewardess.

(Score: deduct one mark per mistake)

16 Commas 3

1   no commas needed
2   no commas needed
3   no commas needed
4   Henry VI, who was only eight months old when he came to the throne in 1422, was England's youngest king.
5   The only British Prime Minister to have been assassinated was Spencer Perceval (1762–1812), who was shot dead when

entering the lobby of the House of Commons.

6 The first woman in space was Valentina Tereshkova of the former Soviet Union, who orbited the Earth in June 1963.

7 Louis Pasteur, whose work on wine, vinegar and beer led to pasteurisation, had an obsessive fear of dirt and infection. He would never shake hands with anybody.

8 The German physicist Wilhelm Konrad Roentgen, who discovered X-rays and initiated a scientific revolution in doing so, refused to apply for any patents in connection with the discovery or to make any financial gains out of it. He died in poverty.

9 The Dutch painter Van Meegeren, who lived from 1899 to 1947, pulled off some of the most brilliant forgeries in art history.

10 'Anthony Edwards has become television's highest-paid actor in a deal which ties him to the hospital drama *ER* for the next four years.
Edwards, who plays Dr Mark Greene, has signed a £21 million contract: equivalent to almost £250,000 an episode. George Clooney, who previously had the largest salary, is leaving the series early next year.'

17 Common spelling errors

I 1 niece, Sheila, pieces, diet
2 ceiling, weird, friend, quiet
II 1 cutlery, medicine
2 conceited, difficult, intelligent

18 Comparisons

I 1 a He is the cleverest person I have ever met.
2 b Honestly, it was the worst day of my life.
3 b If I have to choose between Ahmed and Tariq, I think Ahmed is the better player.
4 a The patient recovered more quickly than expected.
5 b There have been fewer burglaries in this area this year than there were last year.
6 b The film is completely different from the book.

II 1 more neatly
2 neater
3 fewer
4 less
5 fewer
6 better
7 best
8 better
9 worse
10 worse
11 worst

19 Concord

I 1 **Breathing through the lungs**
have, breathe, goes, are, passes, carries, pass, breathe

2 **The cuckoo**
makes, lays, chooses, look, takes, leaves, flies, returns, has, is, hatch, creates,
forces, feeds, cares

3 **The camel**
goes, carries, starts, does, eats, rises, uses

II 1 have
2 has
3 suffers
4 has
5 were
6 are
7 is
8 was
9 are
10 is
11 has
12 were
13 were
14 Has
15 was

20 Dashes (–)

I 1 Bats are not birds – they are mammals.
2 He said he would do it – and he did!
3 There was only one other customer – an untidy, middle-aged man with a pair of binoculars slung over his shoulder.

4 And don't forget – we leave in an hour.
5 He saw the red light in the middle of the road. It was being waved slowly up and down – the international signal to stop.

II 1 Vitamin C – which is essential for healthy teeth, gums and blood vessels – can be found in fresh fruit and vegetables.
2 She and Reg had no secrets from each other. Well – she laughed to herself – only one ...
3 The speed of sound – known as Mach 1, after the Austrian physicist and philosopher Ernst Mach – is different at different heights.
4 The deepest lake in the world – it is nearly a mile deep in places – is Lake Baikal, in Siberia.
5 It wasn't too long ago – 1977, to be exact – that Cairo, a city of 8 million people, had only 208,000 telephones and no telephone directory.

21 Direct speech

I 1 "My doctor has advised me to give up golf," said Fred.
"Why?" asked his friend. "Did he examine your heart?"

"No," replied Fred, "but he had a look at my score card." (. or !)

2 Two small boys were discussing their future.
"What are you going to be when you grow up?" one of them asked.
"A soldier," answered the other.
"What if you get killed?"
"Who would want to kill me?"
"The enemy."
The other boy thought it over.
"Okay," he said. "When I grow up, I'll be the enemy."

II 1 and 3 are correct.
2 and 4 are wrong (no comma needed).

22 Emphatic English

1 Under no circumstances must you touch (or ... are you to touch) those buttons.
2 Not until twenty years later did they find out the truth.
3 By no means is it certain that they will agree to our plan.
4 Much as I respect Renata, I do not think she is the right person for the job.
5 Try as he might, he could not force the door open.
6 Strange as / though it may sound, I don't really want to earn a lot of money.

23 Formal English

1 should
2 shall
3 May
4 whom
5 one, one's, one's

24 Greek and Latin roots

I telephone, telegraph, telescope, microphone, microscope

II 1 manuscript
2 manicure
3 manual
4 scripture(s)
5 We use the term *script* when we refer to the text of a play, film, broadcast or speech. We use the word when referring to a candidate's written answers in an exam. We also use the word when referring to a particular system of writing, e.g. Cyrillic script (used in some Slavonic languages).

III 1 genocide
2 patricide
3 suicide
4 homicide
5 herbicide

25 Homophones

I 1 They're
2 there
3 There

4 their

5 They're, there

II 1 dependent

2 councillor

3 hoard

4 whet

5 playwright

III 1 lifebuoys / life-buoys, quayside, threw

2 taught, knead, dough, bread

3 muscles, beach

4 They're, their, there

5 whole, mourning, died

26 Hyphen (-)

I 1 a fair-haired boy

2 a twelve-year-old girl

3 an eight-hour flight

4 a suspicious-looking man

5 sad-looking eyes

II 1 my great-grandfather

2 possible, but not necessary

3 a break-in

4 possible, but not necessary

5 a hold-up

6 forty-four chairs

7 his ex-wife

8 a non-smoker

27 Informal English 1

1 I received a lot of / plenty of presents from my cousin.

2 He cheated me out of £10.

3 It's fortunate we booked our tickets early.

4 I usually have a bath just before I go to bed.

5 If you won the lottery, what would you do?

6 The test was very easy.

7 She's rather arrogant.

8 You should stand up for your principles.

9 She told him to keep to the point.

10 He asked us to wait for a while.

28 Informal English 2

1 *There are* plenty of things that you can do.

2 You should *have* told me earlier.

3 When he was questioned by the police, he said he hadn't seen *anything* (or ... he *had* seen nothing).

4 *Barry and I* went swimming on Saturday.

5 We went (down) *to* the park for a game of football.

6 I thought he would find the test very difficult, but he did it *really quickly* and without a single mistake.

7 My mother and I *were* walking down the road when we heard a piercing shriek behind us.

8 If I *were* you, I'd see a doctor.

9 *As* I've said before, I don't see why I should help her.

10 Trevor definitely took the money. I *saw* him do it.

29 Informal English 3

1 It's not the cost *that* worries me, it's the time it will take.
2 The thing *that* annoys me is the way she talks about me behind my back.
3 It's no use *my* telling him. He never listens to me.
4 He said he would show me *a quicker way* of doing it.
5 *Fewer* than a hundred people attended the concert.
6 "My daughter's happiness is all *that* matters," he said.
7 I have never *done* and would never do such a thing!
8 No sooner had I watered the plants in the garden *than* it began to rain.

30 Irregular verbs

I The verbs in 1 and 3 are in the present tense.
The verbs in 2 and 4 are in the past tense.

II
1 forbade
2 strove
3 lay
4 laid, began
5 misled
6 stung, flung
7 struck, broke
8 sought
9 stank
10 swam, clung, swept, seen

31 Loan words

I 1 e; 2 b; 3 g; 4 a; 5 f; 6 i; 7 h; 8 c; 9 d.

II AD = in the year of Our Lord (used in the Christian calendar when referring to any year or century after Jesus Christ was born)
a.m. = before midday (in the morning)
e.g. = for example
etc. = and the rest / and so on
i.e. = that is
NB = note well
p.m. = after midday (afternoon / evening / night)
PS = postscript (used to introduce extra words added to the end of a letter or a message)
RIP = (May he / she) rest in peace

32 Loose English

I 1 "Would you mind if I *used* your bathroom?" she asked. / "*Do* you mind if I use your bathroom?" she asked.
2 The reason (why) he is so tired is *that* he has not had a proper break for years.
3 She has a more interesting job than he *has*.

4 She can type faster *than I can*.

5 France is three times *as large* as England.

6 She was *sitting* by the window, reading a magazine.

II 1 Katie is sensible, so I'm sure she will not do anything foolish. / Being a sensible girl / person / child, Katie will not do anything foolish.

2 Since / As it was such a miserable morning, we decided not to go to the beach.

3 Correct.

4 Since / As Ms Hodgkins had suggested the idea in the first place, Mr Fowler could not understand why she had then objected to the plan.

33 Negative prefixes

I 1 disused
2 unused
3 misused
4 disinterested
5 uninterested

II 1 im
2 in
3 mis
4 dis
5 ir
6 im
7 ir
8 in
9 dis
10 mis

34 Nouns 1

I 1 Conqueror
2 director, conductor, actors
3 transistor
4 objectors
5 inventor
6 explorer, navigator
7 calendar
8 Emperor, competitor

II 1 disappearance
2 hindrance
3 maintenance
4 excellence
5 admittance

35 Nouns 2

I 1 competition
2 pronunciation
3 recognition
4 opposition
5 description
6 explanation

II 1 curiosity
2 responsibility
3 humour
4 anxiety
5 strength

III 1 permission
2 collision
3 possession
4 explosion
5 revision

36 Passive voice

1 are known; is estimated
2 is believed; were advertised; was played

3 was covered

4 is covered

5 is known; are still read and referred to

6 was launched; was designed; was knighted

37 Plain English

I 1 d; 2 b; 3 a; 4 f; 5 g; 6 i

II All five statements mean "You are fired!".

38 Plurals

I 1 Zoos

2 Kangaroos

3 mice

4 Tomatoes

5 heroes

6 Rhinos

7 mosquitos / mosquitoes

8 volcanos / volcanoes

II a herd of oxen

a gang of workmen

a gaggle of geese

a flock of sheep

a set of false teeth

39 Prepositions

I 1 Please keep this to yourself. This is strictly between you and *me*.

2 The new committee will *consist of* / *comprise* ten members: seven students and three teachers.

3 For me, the beauty of this poem consists *in* its unusual imagery.

4 Glass is made *from* sand.

5 The criminal's plan was to substitute fake diamonds *for* the ones he intended to steal.

6 You have got away with it so far, but they will catch you *in* the end.

II 1 of

2 off

3 of

4 out of

5 into

6 into

7 off

8 out of

9 out of

10 into

40 Regular verbs in the past

sipped, studied, admitted, envied, incurred, transferred, drawled, occurred, replied, happened, carried, begged, forced, offered, harmed, ordered, kidnapped, travelled, muttered

41 Relative pronouns

1 which

2 who

3 which

4 who

5 whose

6 Who

7 whom

8 who

42 Semicolons (;)

1 'Advice is seldom welcome; and those who want it the most always like it the least.'

2 Chess is one of the oldest games in the world; so old in fact that no one knows who invented it.

43 Spoken and written English

I 1 He is someone in whom I have complete faith.

2 I didn't see anybody. / I saw nobody.

3 She doesn't know. / She does not know.

4 Susan, Ayesha, Sarah, Kiran and I went ... .

5 My brother and I go swimming every Saturday.

II 1 "I don't know who did it."

2 "I want to be a pop star."

3 "Who's / Who is going to tell her?"

4 "I've got to go now. / I have (got) to go now."

5 "Are you all right?"

8 an English dictionary

44 Starting and finishing a sentence

Come and enjoy a relaxing holiday at the Dolphin Hotel. It is very near a clean beach and there are plenty of shops nearby. The hotel is situated in a quiet area and has its own large swimming pool.

The rooms are spacious and clean, and each one has its own private bath and shower with hot and cold water. There is a colour TV in each room and a telephone if you want to call room service.

Our staff are friendly and we offer a high level of service. You will find everybody helpful and cheerful. There is always someone at the reception desk to help you with any problems.

The hotel has two lifts. There is a lounge with comfortable armchairs and a wide selection of newspapers and magazines.

45 Suffixes

I 1 happening
2 fulfilling
3 equipped
4 equipment
5 instalment

II 1 winning, losing
2 waited, cooled, begged
3 writing, planning
4 hoping, hopping
5 tried, slipped
6 tapping, biting
7 yawned, rubbed

46 Tricky verbs

1 lie
2 laid
3 raised

4 risen
5 teaching
6 hung
7 were
8 were
9 doesn't

47 Unnecessary words

1 Omit *on all sides*. Omit *thick* or *dense* and the comma.
2 Omit *atrocious* and *back*
3 Omit *and out of work* and *a period of*.
4 Omit *and every*. Omit *free* or *complimentary*.
5 Omit *nevertheless*
6 Omit *Past*
7 Omit *immediately*
8 Omit *and split*
9 Omit *and significance*
10 Omit *literally*

48 Word endings 1

1 unbearable
2 sociable
3 invincible
4 terrible
5 impossible
6 unavoidable
7 horrible, inedible
8 inflammable
9 illegible

49 Word endings 2

1 dependent
2 dependant
3 independent
4 descendant

5 current
6 attendant
7 relevant
8 insistent
9 accident
10 confident
11 arrogant
12 fire-resistant
13 significant
14 fluent

50 Word endings 3

1 laboratory
2 battery
3 vocabulary
4 bravery
5 slippery
6 injury
7 military
8 missionary
9 cemetery
10 directory

51 Word endings 4

1 ferocious
2 virus
3 notorious
4 spontaneous
5 ludicrous
6 self-conscious
7 atrocious
8 ambitious

52 Words 1

1 Thank you
2 already
3 all ready
4 altogether
5 anyone

6 everyone
7 every day
8 may be

53 Words 2

1 merciful
2 successful
3 beautiful
4 pitiful
5 careful

Appendix 1
Confusing words 1

1 affect
2 illusion
3 appreciable
4 compliment
5 envelope
6 eminent
7 illicit
8 eluded
9 inquiry
10 ingenious

Confusing words 2

infer, morale, respectfully, especially, access, stationery, regrettable, principal, loath, disinterested, later, You're

Confusing words 3

1 flair
2 afflicts
3 broach

4 emigrate
5 bated
6 flouting
7 filing
8 sometime
9 heroin
10 luxuriant

Confusing words 4

1 authoritarian
2 emotive
3 definitive
4 odious
5 contemptible
6 deceased
7 effective
8 deficient
9 urban
10 quite, dessert

Appendix 2
Words ending in *-k*, *-ck*, and *-ke*

1 snack
2 snake
3 lick
4 back
5 bake

Appendix 3
Some problems of usage

1 number
2 besides
3 personnel
4 imaginative
5 classical

Knowledge check answer key

Adjectives

I
1. hungry
2. angry, horrible
3. awful, wonderful
4. wavy, rosy
5. straight
6. cheerful, nasty
7. noisy
8. stony, rough
9. difficult, runny, terrible
10. tasty
11. possible
12. painful, necessary

II
A. inefficient; uneven; ungrateful; inexpensive; inconvenient; unfair; incurable; inaccurate; informal; unusual
B. impolite; unpopular; unpleasant; impatient
C. irresponsible; unreliable; illegible; unreasonable; unlucky; illiterate
D. disobedient; unsatisfactory; disrespectful; disloyal; unfortunate

III
1. smaller, lighter
2. biggest, taller
3. saltier
4. thinner, harder
5. busiest
6. hottest, driest, coldest, windiest
7. widest
8. smallest, largest

Adverbs

I
1. immediately
2. angrily
3. accidentally
4. incredibly
5. fantastically
6. completely
7. probably
8. desperately
9. terribly
10. possibly
11. usually
12. Suddenly
13. happily
14. Unfortunately
15. normally

II
1. He responded sympathetically to her request.
2. They argue occasionally, like all couples.
3. He said that they had to surrender unconditionally.
4. She behaved unpredictably.
5. I had originally planned to have a very quiet wedding.
6. His proposal was criticised heavily by everybody concerned. / His proposal was heavily criticised by everybody concerned.
7. They struggled heroically against impossible odds.
8. He was fatally injured.
9. The fire was probably caused by an electrical fault.
10. She died peacefully.

11 The cost of petrol has risen dramatically.
12 They suffered terribly.
13 She, very sensibly, called the police. (Alternatively, we could say: Very sensibly, she called the police.)
14 He looked at her angrily. / He looked angrily at her.
15 Although he apologised profusely, she would not forgive him.

American and British spelling

1 dialled
2 moustache
3 analysing
4 draught
5 pyjamas
6 jewellery
7 archaeologist
8 instalments
9 through
10 haemorrhage
11 equalled
12 sceptical

Apostrophes 1

I don't
I'm, wasn't
can't

II 1 doesn't
2 They're
3 That's
4 There's
5 it's
6 Who's
7 I've
8 She's
9 weren't
10 shouldn't

Apostrophes 2

I 1 They've, fortnight's
2 they'd, weeks'
3 Mrs Brown's, vet's
4 Here's, ladies', men's
5 There's, We'd
6 wasn't, Aicha's, couldn't
7 They're
8 Let's, newsagent's
9 parents'
10 That's, son's, Where's, James's / James'

II A 1 Who's
2 Whose
3 Whose
4 Who's

B 1 its
2 It's
3 It's
4 its, its

C 1 There's
2 theirs
3 theirs
4 There's

III 1 yours
2 hers
3 his
4 theirs
5 ours

as and like

1 like
2 as if
3 as
4 as
5 like
6 as
7 as
8 like
9 as

10 as if
11 as if
12 As
13 as if
14 like

Capital letters

1 For many years it was thought that the Nile was the longest river in the world. In 1969, however, it was finally decided that the mighty Amazon in South America was 4,195 miles long, fifty more than the Nile.
2 When Sir Walter Raleigh introduced tabacco into England in the early 1600's, King James I wrote a booklet arguing against its use.
3 "Have you met Professor Oshima? He's a very famous professor from Tokyo."
4 My eldest brother is studying Economics at Essex University. When I leave school, I'm going to be a hairdresser.
5 My brother, Tony, is a doctor. He lives in Wales and he speaks Welsh fluently. We usually see him at Christmas and sometimes, at Easter.

Colons (:)

1 The whole area was dark and deserted: no street lights, no house lights, nothing.
2 She had been smoking marijuana and taking other drugs since she was thirteen. Now, said Mrs Turner, she had gone on to something worse: heroin.

3 When I got to the top, I saw a most spectacular sight: five dragons were fighting five unicorns.
4 The notice said: 'Private. Keep out!'
5 Samir can't come with us: he's not old enough.
6 There was still one problem: how were we going to get back in time?
7 And then I had a happy thought: there was no school tomorrow.
8 One person, the American inventor Thomas Midgley (1889-1944), created what are considered to be two of today's biggest environmental evils: chlorofluorocarbons (CFCs) and leaded petrol.

Commas 1

1 The moon has no atmosphere and no water, so no life is possible.
2 If air is blown into water, bubbles rise to the surface.
3 People have been mining gold, silver, tin, iron, copper and lead for thousands of years.
4 Scientists have discovered that bees, mosquitoes, wasps and other stinging insects prefer to sting girls rather than boys.
5 The giraffe is the tallest of all living animals, but scientists are unable to explain how it got its long neck.
6 One of the things that birds, snakes, frogs, cows and humans all have in common is a backbone.

7 Even after their heads have been cut off, some insects may live for as long as a year. They react automatically to light, temperature, humidity and other stimuli.

8 Although I have been to France several times, I do not speak French.

9 According to legend, a mermaid is a young girl who lives in the sea. Instead of legs, she has the tail of a fish.

10 With the exception of the organ, the piano is the most complex musical instrument.

11 With the possible exception of the cobra, crocodiles kill more people than any other animal.

12 She opened the parcel, saw what was inside and let out a shrill scream.

13 According to Yoko, Fusako intends to sell her cottage and move back to the city.

14 We yawn when we are tired, sleepy or bored.

Commas 2

1 Among the most important peoples of ancient America were the Aztecs, who lived in the valley in which Mexico City is situated.

2 no commas required

3 The Vatican City, which is the official home of the Pope, is the world's smallest country.

4 Penicillin, which was discovered by Alexander Fleming, has saved millions of lives.

5 Silver, which is a precious metal, is lighter than gold.

6 The human body has 636 muscles, each with its own name.

7 The St Gotthard tunnel, which runs beneath the Swiss Alps, is the world's longest road tunnel.

8 no commas required

9 no commas required

10 He wanted to give all his money to charity, which seemed very reasonable to me.

11 no commas required

12 no commas required

13 The 'Mona Lisa', which was painted by Leonardo da Vinci, is the most easily recognised painting in the world.

14 My father, who used to be a businessman, is training to be a bus driver.

Commas 3

1 The Austrialian Aborigines were the earliest-known inhabitants of Australia. The term *aborigine,* which comes from the Latin words *ab origine,* means 'from the beginning'.

2 Australia is one of the world's leading exporters of sugarcane, which grows along the north-eastern coast.

3 The Arctic is dominated by the Arctic Ocean and a vast treeless plain called the tundra. Unlike Antarctica, which is an ice-covered continent, much of the Arctic consists of ice-covered seas.

4 Lake Baikal, which is located in Siberia, is the only lake in the world that is deep enough to have deep-sea fish.

5   no commas needed
6   Unlike chess and draughts, which are very ancient games, the game of dominoes is comparatively new.

Common spelling errors

I   know, fetch, solemn, stitching, straight, answered, conscious, friend, business, could, whisper, ghastly, strength, conscience, scratching, acquired, acquitted, secretary, kneeling

II   library; luggage; necessary; occasionally; opportunity parallel; professional; recommend; successful; scissors; surprised; foreign; collision; particularly; accident

Comparisons

1   laziest
2   healthier, fitter
3   quietly
4   best-looking, cleverest
5   more efficiently
6   slowest, more quickly
7   earlier

Concord

1   is
2   are
3   was
4   wants
5   costs
6   was
7   are
8   have, has

9   is
10   eats, is
11   are
12   is
13   are
14   is

Dashes (–)

I   1   Even at that early hour – it was not yet six o'clock – he was immaculately dressed.
2   Everything that we know about dinosaurs – and everything that we will ever know – comes from fossils.
3   An unusual thing about the spotted hyena is that – unlike most animals – the female is larger than the male.
4   How could you speak to him – your own father – in such a way?
5   Even my brother – who is not known for his sense of humour – had to laugh when I told him what had happened.

II   1   The longest jump that has ever been recorded was a great bound of forty-two feet made by a kangaroo back in 1951 – though, of course, it cannot be proved that there have not been even longer unrecorded ones.
2   He was a tall, lean man with thinning hair and a pleasant face – the kind of face one would find hard to remember.
3   He smiled again – a cold, hard smile.

4   An iceberg larger than Belgium was observed in the South Pacific in 1956. It was 208 miles long and 60 miles wide – the largest ever seen.

5   The longest underwater cable is nine thousand miles long, and it runs all the way from Australia to Port Alberni, Canada. It is known as COMPAC – the Commonwealth Pacific Cable.

Direct speech

He looked at her and said, "Where did you get that from?"
"I found it," she said. "It was on the floor."
"I don't believe you!" he shouted at the top of his voice.
"There's no need to shout," she said in a firm voice.
"Give it to me," he growled, "or you'll be sorry!"

Emphatic English

1   It was because of his greed that he lost everything.

2   Nowhere else in the world will you find such generous and spontaneous hospitality.

3   So shocking was the news that nobody knew what to say.

4   At no time did we suspect that the money had been stolen.

5   Only later did they tell me about it.

6   Strange as / though it may seem, he quite likes being in prison.

7   Much as I admire her courage, I think it was foolish of her to go there on her own.

8   Good as / though he may be at languages, he is hopeless at Maths.

Formal English

1   She was introduced to a man called Smith, *whom* she vaguely recognised.

2   *No* change

3   'Almost all absurdity of conduct arises from the imitation of those *whom* we cannot resemble.' (Samuel Johnson)

Greek and Latin roots

I   dictaphone, dictate, dictation, dictator, diction, dictionary addict, contradict, edict, predict, verdict

II   1   arch-rivals
     2   pseudo-intellectual
     3   hypersensitive
     4   Claustrophobia
     5   retrospect
     6   foretell
     7   anti-war
     8   hyperactive
     9   pseudonym
    10   foregone

Homophones

I   1   past
    2   whether
    3   pale
    4   fir
    5   software
    6   formally
    7   poured
    8   grateful

1 too
2 break
3 rain, plain
4 stationery
5 which
6 prey
7 Whose
8 flee
9 sole
10 alter
11 hangars
12 minor
13 sight
14 write, foreword
15 prise
16 cereal
17 idol
18 sore

Hyphens (-)

1 ill- tempered, pig-headed, hard-hearted
2 silver-coloured
3 grey-bearded, middle-aged
4 thick-set, pleasant-looking, mid-thirties
5 one-eyed, serious-looking
6 home-baked
7 seventeenth-century, extra-large, three-month
8 husband-to-be, hard-headed, multi-storey
9 ten-year-old
10 sitting-room

Irregular verbs

1 caught, found, got
2 stung, hurt
3 thought, lost, fought, won
4 spread, burst
5 held, slid
6 kept

7 bent, split
8 taught
9 stuck, made
10 spent, built, could

Loose English

I 1 a She has better eyesight than I have.
   b She can see better than I can.
2 The model car is four times as expensive as the model aeroplane.
3 The reason (why) we are thinking of moving is that we are not satisfied with any of the schools in our area.
4 Would it be all right if we postponed the meeting until tomorrow?

II 1 *sitting* not *sat*
2 correct
3 *sitting* not *sat*
4 correct

Negative prefixes

1 disappoint
2 unofficial
3 unnoticed
4 disagreed
5 disobey
6 Irregular
7 illiterate
8 inadvisable
9 misused
10 disloyal

Nouns 1

I 1 a translator
2 a smuggler
3 grammar

4 a traitor
5 a solicitor
6 a lawyer
7 a radiator
8 an announcer
9 a spectator
10 a caterpillar
11 a liar
12 a doctor
13 a sailor
14 a collar
15 a dictator
16 a prisoner
17 a visitor
18 a word-processor
19 an author
20 a burglar

II
1 a survivor
2 a beggar
3 an inspector
4 vinegar
5 an editor
6 a gardener
7 a governor
8 a ventilator
9 a computer
10 a thermometer

III
1 Absence
2 acquaintances
3 repentance
4 endurance
5 substance
6 Silence
7 influence
8 performances
9 experience
10 difference
11 conference, audience, ignorance

Nouns 2

1 happiness
2 friendliness
3 achievement
4 ugliness
5 excitement
6 dizziness, dryness

Passive voice

1 Sometimes shining coloured lights, called aurorae, can be seen in the skies above the North and South Poles.
2 Wild animals have been kept in zoos since ancient times.
3 Ice hockey is considered to be the fastest game in the world.
4 It is said that Mark Twain wrote most of his books in bed. / Mark Twain is said to have written most of his books in bed.
5 The election has been postponed until next month.
6 The study of fossils is called paleontology.
7 In India the cow is regarded as a sacred animal.
8 Smoking is not allowed/ permitted in this area.
9 Owls of one species or another are found in all parts of the world.
10 In ancient times, the owl was thought to be an unlucky bird.

Plain English

1 How well does he get on with his colleagues?
2 He shows little initiative. / He is not very creative.
3 As suppliers of bureau services, our company's aim is to be one of the best in the field. We are seeking capable individuals to help us fulfil this aim.

4 He is a good manager.
5 My father is a furniture salesman.
6 My brother is short for his age.
7 I am afraid that Mr Wilkins has died.
8 Innocent civilians died as a result of the missile attack.

Plurals

I 1 wolves
2 elves, goblins, fairies
3 stories
4 witches
5 cities, villages
6 Octopuses
7 wives
8 sandwiches, bunches, bananas, sausages, biscuits

Prepositions

1 in
2 of
3 at
4 composed
5 in
6 from
7 of
8 of
9 in
10 on
11 In, with
12 to
13 at
14 with
15 I
16 me
17 from
18 to
19 with

Regular verbs in the past

stared, recognised, starred, enjoyed, worshipped, recalled, quarrelled, cancelled, ruined, wondered, preferred, reminded, fulfilled, hesitated, pulled, shuffled, opened

Relative pronouns

1 which
2 which
3 which
4 who
5 whose
6 who
7 whom
8 which
9 whose
10 whom

Starting and finishing a sentence

I Snakes are cold-blooded creatures. They are only as hot or cold as the air around them. That is why you don't find many snakes in cool countries such as Britain. It's simply too chilly for them to stay alive.

II 1 What is her name?
2 What a surprise!
3 How embarrassing!
4 How did it happen?
5 Do you know the answer?
6 Do it now!

Suffixes

I 1 spotted, banned, taped, tapped, rowed, cried, played,

slapped, popped, hummed, peered, peeped

2 digging, slimming, heating, hitting, running, sewing, sweating, gazing, flying, shining, staring, starring

3 greater, bigger, thinner, fatter, cooler, mixer, wetter, waiter, mugger, robber, printer

4 fastest, saddest, largest, latest, nicest, driest, hottest

5 deafen, rotten, sadden, woollen, wooden, madden, soften, gladden

6 reddish, snobbish, bluish, foolish, childish

II 1 committed, referred, offered, cancelled, appealed, panicked

2 preferring, quarrelling, concealing, developing, benefitting, beginning

3 occurrence, reference, preference, excellence, difference

4 installation, cancellation, imagination, limitation, transportation

Unnecessary words

1 Omit *and completely*.
2 Omit *and truly*.
3 Omit *of twos*.
4 Omit *again*.
5 Omit *and damp*.
6 Omit *different* and the final word *(speech)*.
7 Omit *at any time*.
8 Omit *the course of* and, if you wish, *of the* before *horses*.
9 Omit *Personally*.
10 Omit *in person*.
11 Omit *back*.

12 Omit *for that reason*.
13 Omit *in the morning*.
14 Omit *and errors* and *again*.
15 Omit *unexpected* and change *an* to *a*.
16 Omit *back*.
17 Omit *quickly*.
18 Omit *on foot*.
19 Omit *and brief*.
20 Omit *whole*.

Tricky verbs

1 lie
2 lay
3 laid
4 lying
5 raise
6 rises
7 teaching
8 hanged
9 hung
10 were
11 were, was
12 were
13 doesn't
14 doesn't

Word endings 1

responsible; sensible; advisable; available; incredible; irritable; flexible; possible; reliable; visible

Word endings 2

1 instant
2 elegant
3 current
4 persistent, truant
5 pleasant
6 reluctant
7 incident

8 magnificent
9 permanent
10 urgent
11 excellent
12 brilliant, ignorant
13 convenient
14 expectant
15 eminent
16 present
17 observant
18 applicant, vacant
19 insolent
20 lenient
21 blackcurrant
22 reliant

Word endings 3

1 dictionary
2 library
3 advisory
4 confectionery
5 primary
6 February
7 temporary
8 compulsory
9 summary
10 itinerary
11 perjury
12 memory
13 extraordinary
14 victory
15 anniversary
16 secretary
17 solitary
18 predatory
19 scenery
20 adultery
21 tributary
22 estuary
23 contrary
24 Hungary
25 hereditary
26 territory
27 lavatory

Word endings 4

1 fictitious
2 contagious
3 oblivious
4 octopus
5 vicious
6 suspicious
7 hideous
8 luxurious
9 previous
10 instantaneous
11 pretentious
12 conscientious

Words 1

1 altogether
2 Any one
3 any one
4 anyone
5 Every one
6 no one, Everyone
7 every day
8 already
9 all ready
10 Maybe
11 may be
12 may be
13 any way
14 thank you
15 in front
16 in case
17 cannot
18 supermarket
19 flatmate

Words 2

1 almost
2 already
3 harmful
4 pastime
5 fulfil

6 skilful, graceful
7 altogether
8 grandson, handful
9 earrings / ear-rings
10 farewell, sorrowful, tearfully, until

11 principle
12 stationery
13 moral
14 implying
15 correct
16 especially
17 latter

Appendix 1
Confusing words 1

1 correct
2 effect
3 affecting
4 correct
5 adverse
6 illusion
7 appreciative
8 appreciable
9 complement
10 corps
11 correct
12 imminent
13 elicit
14 eludes
15 correct
16 correct
17 implicit
18 human
19 inhumane
20 ingenuous

Confusing words 2

1 inferred
2 morale
3 respectively
4 regretful
5 specially
6 stationary
7 uninterested
8 principles
9 correct
10 loath / loth

Confusing words 3

1 inflicted
2 some time, sometime
3 filing
4 flare
5 forgotten, left
6 brooch
7 flaunt
8 flair
9 baited
10 sometime
11 inflict
12 luxurious
13 heroine
14 baiting
15 afflicted
16 flout

Confusing words 4

1 emotional
2 authoritarian
3 contemptible
4 diseased
5 efficient
6 urbane
7 defective
8 desert, unawares
9 inflammable
10 definitive, authoritative
11 emotive
12 odious
13 erotic
14 contemptuous
15 deceased

Appendix 2

Words ending in *-k, -ck* and *-ke*

1 joking
2 rake
3 knocked
4 packet
5 chicken
6 jacket
7 tricks
8 shocked
9 broke
10 breakfast

Appendix 3

Problems of usage

1 quite
2 where
3 dessert
4 envelope
5 consist
6 lightning
7 tolerant
8 trusting
9 lonely